T0193428

Let there be light.

THE FUTURE OF
MEDICINE AND HEALTH CARE

INTEGRATIVE HOLISTIC TEAM
PREVENTION, DIAGNOSIS, AND TREATMENT

ELIMINATE DEATH BY HARMFUL DRUGS AND UNNECESSARY SURGERY.
THE BODY HEALS ITSELF... DOCTORS DO NOT.
SYMPTOMS ARE A MESSAGE... LOCATE AND TREAT THE CAUSES!

DR. WALTER J. URBAN WITH ALEXANDRA LUTY

authorHOUSE®

AuthorHouse™
1663 Liberty Drive
Bloomington, IN 47403
www.authorhouse.com
Phone: 1 (800) 839-8640

Published by AuthorHouse 06/13/2019

ISBN: 978-1-7283-1407-5 (sc)
ISBN: 978-1-7283-1405-1 (hc)
ISBN: 978-1-7283-1406-8 (e)

Library of Congress Control Number: 2019942707

Print information available on the last page.

Any people depicted in stock imagery provided by Getty Images are models, and such images are being used for illustrative purposes only. Certain stock imagery © Getty Images.

This book is printed on acid-free paper.

Because of the dynamic nature of the Internet, any web addresses or links contained in this book may have changed since publication and may no longer be valid. The views expressed in this work are solely those of the author and do not necessarily reflect the views of the publisher, and the publisher hereby disclaims any responsibility for them.

CONTENTS

DEDICATION

To the memory of my mother who died during surgery and to those who will open their minds to saving the future children and the health of the planet. This book, in addition to my last three, has been written to help people. That is what I am here for. My heart feels good when I am helping, and I feel joy when people receive my help. I understand and accept people where they are. This allows me to have compassion for them and to want to help.

I hope that you open your mind to helping yourself. Let go of old beliefs that are not really helping you and go beyond your present self-limiting thoughts, ideas, speech and actions. I send you all my love.

A great big thank you to Alexandra Luty for all that she has done to help me write this book.

FOREWORD

By Alexandra Luty

It is my strong and sincere opinion that opportunities presenting themselves to us must be seized. Such was the case when I saw a social media posting by an author who I recently wrote an article about asking if there's anyone who would like to work with him to create a life-changing health book for the modern age. As someone who is fairly new to writing published works and even newer to caring for my health, I saw this as a call directed to me. This was my opportunity to work with an established author and to go through the process of researching, writing, editing and publishing a complete work. What I didn't realize at the time, though, was that I wouldn't just be learning—I would be changing, too.

The following book is ready to challenge the accepted, mainstream models of tackling the problems faced by humanity. And it will do so with very little effort—just a complete dissolution of how we frame our problems in the first place. The ideas in this book will destroy the egos that have been clouding the dialogue about why humans become unhealthy in the first place. It will destroy them, only to rebuild them again—this time with love and proper support. Life is not created in a vacuum. Neither are the problems that plague life. There is a root to every problem and a reason for every symptom. Although it may not be obvious from the surface level, we build our bodies and our world with our thoughts, emotions, actions and reactions. It's time that patients, medical doctors and health care practitioners, from all modalities, took responsibility for their personal continued education and put aside their immutable professional egos.

Each of us is blessed to have our own journey that is filled with individual experiences. Every 'healing facilitator' encounters their own personal set of maladies that come to their professional attention. Each of these experiences lends itself to gathering a set of knowledge with which they go on to treat their patients. The goal of this book is to push doctors to go beyond their personal knowledge base by talking with other practitioners more often and crowdsourcing more answers from within their own medical community, or even from the wider, global health care communities. When it becomes purely obvious that all of us have room to grow—even those at the top of their profession—we will put our individual egos in their balanced place and begin to heal as a planet.

There are parts of our world that the scientific community still does not understand. Scientists are still discovering new functions inside the human body in the 21st century. There is likely no subject that we have studied for longer than the human body and yet the full extent of its processes are sometimes a mystery to the top minds of today. After all of the experiments that have ever been conducted on human subjects, doctors are only beginning to understand the placebo effect and why patients who get no treatment or sham treatment recover at the same rate as those receiving test treatments[1]. We realize that the mind plays a role in the recovery of the body but it feels as though scientists have not been looking with much effort to prove how or why that role comes into the picture. If they did, they would recognize that the body works as a team of different parts that require their own, individual attention to make them function optimally as a whole. This means that medical practitioners of different varieties are needed to help the body find the equilibrium it needs to heal itself.

Instead of looking into the root causes of disease and listening to their patients' individual stories, medical doctors are largely relying on their streamlined educations that are packed full of the most peer-reviewed (and most privately funded) research about what modern science thinks it knows about the human body. Never mind the gaps in the official stories of our human health. Never mind the individual anecdotes that match up alongside causes pointed to by individual patients. Modern, allopathic

---

[1] http://time.com/5392687/placebo-effect-pain/

medicinal science wants us to believe that it knows best about what to do with our symptoms. They give us antidotes and even vaccines to prevent what supposedly ails us: our symptoms of pain and discomfort. Surely, I can believe that they might know how to accomplish these goals. But to me, that kind of 'might' is not enough. What is better than modern medicine's "best information" is *all* of the information about health and healing. And the only way to get all of the information is to come together and share in our collective pool of knowledge. This means that doctors need to listen to their patients who come to them describing why they think that they are having symptoms. Doctors must also listen to their fellow practitioners, of all modalities, to learn the right questions to ask their patients in order to get the full picture. And patients must ask all of their intuitive questions and bring forth their personal experiences, while also being ready to listen, think and learn.

If the mind really does play a role in our ability to heal the causes of our disease, then science can take some cues from belief. It's time to believe that none of us has all of the answers. We don't even have all of the questions. Our egos may not want to believe but our egos can no longer rule on their own. The human heart has its own mini brain with which it rules over some of the most important processes in the human body. Of course, neither the heart or the brain can exist without the other. It's no wonder that the heart symbolically represents love—the closest representation of symbiotic closeness that linguists and philosophers have devised. We must pay attention to the body with our analytical minds and our open hearts at the same time. It's time to take everything into consideration all at once. No matter how hard it may seem to be, if we're all in it together, there is no failure that we cannot accept and move forward.

***

Working on this manuscript with Dr. Urban has shifted my perspective by challenging me to be more honest with myself about my health. No longer do I blink things away, pretending that I don't know that drinking a Coca Cola will not only injure my health in the long run, but that by drinking it, I am supporting an industry that poisons environments and economies. I can no longer sit idly without asking myself if I've had enough exercise that day, or if I've stretched enough, or meditated enough, rather than staring at my smart phone. These are not revolutionary ideas. Instead, this has been an evolution of consciousness to a state of more integrity. By questioning my thoughts, ideas, and actions more regularly and methodically, I am becoming more honest and possibly more myself. I'm not lying to myself anymore, so there is no need to divide my attention or divert my mind while I think or perform things that I know to be harmful.

This book has been challenging to write in more ways than one. If I take anything away from this experience, it will be to look before I leap from now on. Jumping on an opportunity can be a blessed experience, but knowing where you are jumping to and what it will feel like when you land really brings a whole new dimension of fearlessness to the experience. Fear may be a powerful motivator for some, but to me, knowledge is the real power.

I hope that you find power in the experience of reading this book as much as I have in helping create it. What you do with this information is entirely in your hands. But if this book has even half the power that I know it to have, I have no doubt that it will change your life, too.

Seize the opportunities presented to you here. Just remember to look before you leap.

FOREWORD

By Dr. Carolina Ortega Ballesteros, MD

Life advances by leaps and bounds, every day we see more situations that make us think about the future of nature and therefore the future of the human race. The scenarios are terrifying, but more frightening is that we are not able to stop along the way and at least try to act according to what our heart or instinct says.

Many times we have been told about the importance of maintaining good health, but experts have taught us little about how to achieve it. Do you know why? Because experts have the last word on this subject.

Sitting once as a patient in a waiting room, a medical colleague, who had been assigned to assist me, calls my name "Carolina Ortega Ballesteros." I entered his small office and without looking me, he offered to sit me down. After a few minutes of looking at the screen of his computer, he asked "what is your reason for consultation?" At that time, I still had not seen his eyes. I answered: I have felt a little pain in the pit of my stomach since several months ago. A doctor prescribed me antacids like omeprazole and I have not gotten better."

Without even taking my blood pressure, my pulse or palpating my abdomen, my colleague hands me an order for an endoscopy of the upper digestive tract. With great sadness and indignation, I try to get his attention by increasing the tone of my voice, with no success.

I left his office and managed to analyze several aspects on my way home that I believe marked my personal and professional life, and how they differ from my colleague's treatment of me as a patient:

1. You never know of whom you are in front. All human beings are equal and we need the compassion and support of the doctor when we visit them.
2. Health programs worldwide are so systematized and so fragmented that they only allow us to observe and alleviate symptoms, without seeing the whole.
3. The doctor who took care of me is sicker than me and perhaps not satisfied with the demands to which he is subjected daily in his work, or by the personal situations that he carries in his suitcase.
4. The cause of the disease is multifactorial and we should not focus only on the body. Mind and spirit also intervene.
5. The emotion that the doctor generated in me—indignation— worsened the symptoms.
6. Visual contact is essential in any interpersonal relationship.
7. We must change the world; and to do so, we must start with ourselves.

Over time I discovered the cause of my abdominal burning and I can assure you that it was not my stomach.

***

In his book, The Future of Medicine and Health Care, Dr. Walter J Urban manages to capture, in a simple way, and with scientific, technical and experiential foundation, some tools to begin to forge change. The large amount of information available on social networks makes it easier to know if a professional is or is not beneficial for our health and well-being. But we also have irresponsible and sensational electronic sources capable of causing more unresolved questions.

The faculties of medicine form us into working machines, performing shifts of up to 24 hours in an emergency service as a required for the desired degree and authority to be called doctors. They call us doctors and our ego goes up to heaven. They call us doctors and we believe we have the last word. They call us doctors and we do not allow the patient to talk about everything he feels, lives and eats. They call us doctors and we forget our families and dedicate ourselves to be more recognized in the workplace instead.

We continue to call ourselves doctors and yet many of us have forgotten how to really be doctors. Recyclers, lawyers, businessmen, teachers, engineers; most trades create associations in order to fight for the common good. Doctors are trained to be selfish, competitive, and in some cases, with little sensitivity to the pain of others. This is what makes it difficult for us to form multidisciplinary associations for the welfare of the society entrusted to us. It is difficult for the physician to accept that he does not know something about a health issue, and he prefers, on multiple occasions, to affirm that only his knowledge is valid.

If you have the courage to tell the oncologist that you prefer Vitamin C instead of chemotherapy, or even as an adjuvant, for example, your doctor will probably tell you that Vitamin C only serves to treat scurvy and scurvy is an extinct disease on our planet. Without any scientific information justifying that response, the doctor is able to stay in their position, just by keeping a mind closed and feeding their ego.

We must be the 'health professional pioneers' of the long-awaited change that translates well-being to future generations, starting by throwing away obsolete mental paradigms that only make us involute. The professional practice of alternative medicine changed my life and I do not lose heart in the attempt to change the lives of my patients and their families.

PART 1:

Introduction To Integrative Holistic Team Prevention, Diagnosis And Treatment

"First, do no harm. Let food be your medicine and medicine be your food." —Hippocrates

***

Allopathic medicine has some DANGEROUS treatments. There are harmful drugs and harmful surgeries. Chemotherapy and radiation have extremely adverse effects. These four aspects of harm done by allopathic medicine must be exposed to the public and explained to all patients. Do no harm was the doctor's oath and it must never be forgotten.

A great amount of supporting evidence has proven these four points, yet allopathic practitioners continue to be trained to prescribe these treatments and many are still unaware of their harmful and dangerous effects. They are slaves to their limited education... so limited that they themselves may use the same four treatments. What a tragedy for all involved, except of course those who earn annual huge profits from the misery that these harmful standard allopathic treatments cause!

FROM EVOLUTION TO REVOLUTION

The concept of an integrative holistic team is the first step in what is coming in medicine and health care. Many allopathic medical doctors have made significant changes in their practices in realizing the importance of diet, exercise, sleep, micro- and macro-biomes, etc. Some claim to have found cures for cancer and diabetes, turning away from the modern consensus that chemotherapy, radiation and pharmaceutical drugs are the best options for treatment. Those wanting to try something different are turning to what is generally termed 'alternative medicine,' also known as the original medicine.

Drug companies control allopathic medical schools. According to researchers Rijul Kshirsagar and Priscilla Vu at University of California, Irvine School of Medicine, students receive gifts such as free meals, textbooks, pocket texts, small trinkets and drug samples. They conclude that "forty to 100 percent of medical students report exposure to the pharmaceutical industry, with clinical students being more likely than preclinical students to report exposure."[2] After medical school, the pharmaceutical industry spends at least $5 billion annually on marketing in the US, which is more than $8,000 per physician.[3] Today, big corporations still own the food companies, TV stations, most of the print, online media and insurance companies, while the rest of us continue to live inside a matrix of power created by those who hold the money and assets behind the scenes.

---

[2] http://in-training.org/drugged-greed-pharmaceutical-industrys-role-us-medical-education-10639

[3] http://in-training.org/drugged-greed-pharmaceutical-industrys-role-us-medical-education-10639

This control, however, is going to be eliminated as the public wakes up to the truth of proper lifestyle and environment. The evolution will turn into a revolution and the old medical structure will break apart and collapse. We, the people of the world, want to become and stay healthy as we get more information. We will overcome our fears and what we have been taught. Our numbers are growing and will continue to grow.

NO ONE DIES OF CANCER, HEART ATTACK, DIABETES, OR ANY OTHER DISEASE.

PEOPLE DIE OF BAD LIFESTYLE AND INADEQUATE MEDICINE AND HEALTH CARE!

PREFACE

"Employ your time in improving yourself by other men's writings so that you shall come easily by what others have labored hard for." —Socrates

Amidst all of the competition in the world today, a little cooperation would be nice to see. With this book, we are helping to contribute to the next step in the future of health care by manifesting the creation of an 'Integrative Holistic Team.' We, the team of authors of this book, don't feel the need to wait for an inspired leader, nor do we seek to take up this mantle. It is our goal to share the breadth of our current, common, foundational health care information with the world so that the first teams of inspired practitioners willing to work together can heal patients together. We believe that this team will continue to inspire more teams of its kind, until we reach the tipping point in health care: where modern meets ancient, and alternative meets traditional.

Each of us—patients and practitioners—can do a better job in helping each other. In realizing that many health care practitioners currently compete for their financial survival, it is understandable that it has not been an easy process to allow the space for all modalities to exist in the realm of 'modern medicine'. Many health care theories are still hotly debated today, and more than a few health care practitioners have been banned by various medical authorities around the world for their controversial theories, no matter how widespread or culturally significant a practice may be.

Despite the controversies, the last few decades have seen an increase in the demand for "alternative" medicine. This growth in interest shows us that the patient has become more aware of the available health care options and that the patient is willing to follow their intuition; to take a chance on something new (or old). And there is good reason for this.

In 1978, I wrote the book <u>Integrative Therapy: Foundation for Holistic and Self-Healing</u> about the 'health care team' concept. It was called a "breakthrough book" and "the first of its kind" in reviews from my peers. This book defined the idea of 'Integrative Therapy'—the breakthrough idea that healing is more important than the theory or method used to heal. With the addition of the term 'prevention' to the title of this book, the content of the following treatise becomes unique and a great step forward in health care integration and ultimately healing.

Since the creation of the Internet, humans have begun moving beyond a history confined by the fragmentation of information. A thirst for more information has pervaded the health care industry. Now is the time to do it. We are ready! Read this book with an open and inquisitive mind and you will benefit from the reduction of human suffering at the hands of a lack of information. By understanding how to holistically treat illness, we will come to understand the importance of the whole picture. And vice versa.

For a common definition of a state of enduring health, we propose that a holistic picture includes: a good diet, regular exercise, supplementing our natural deficiencies naturally, and listening to our bodily reactions. With this idea of paying attention to ourselves and to those around us, we are creating the platform for the prevention of disease by treating our bodies as sacred and a part of a larger whole.

Those who think they know a lot learn very little.
Those who know they know very little can learn a lot.

Once Upon A Time

There was an old man who studied and studied and studied. He assumed that he knew something of the world. Some of his friends even thought he knew something. But then after much self-reflection, he began to wonder if he really knew anything at all. He talked about love and thought that all his studies were bringing him to love.

Years later, he realized that talking about love, like he and others did, was equal to speaking empty words. He realized that talking about love was just coming from the mind. And even talking about it with feeling, from the heart and mind together, seemed to make more sense. And after much reflection, he realized that he must also *show* love, to all and everything. Treating others and all with love was the only way to be *in* love.

The people around the old man do not understand that acceptance, compassion and understanding are all a part of the foundation of practicing loving behavior in action. He wonders why this is so? He reflects again and thinks that people are often times emotionally dominated by their life history and cannot give up their their old thoughts, ideas, behaviors and egoic personality. He tries to tell others about this idea but it is not accepted and makes people feel and act defensive. He tries again and again and then finally gives up.

He reflects again and thinks about what he can do.

Then, he awakens, realizes that it was all a dream and goes back to sleep.

PURPOSE

"The beginning is the most important part of the work." —Plato

An Introduction To Integrative Care

The traditional modalities of health care are all limited by their inherent, self-imposed boundaries and by the limits of the practitioner's mind who stays within their learned boundaries. These modalities are no longer the best methods for practitioner or patient. Globally, we fall short of providing the best patient care possible. Patients are often not recovering from long-identified diseases and syndromes and in many cases symptoms progress with or without health care attention. These results can and do lead to hopelessness. In these scenarios, the practitioner often does not grow professionally and often stays in a closed-minded and defensive position.

There is, however, a new breed of health care practitioner; one who is ready to abandon their professional ego in order to grow. This is evidenced by various summits on the Internet like The Sacred Plant series, which discusses the curative benefits of medicinal cannabis use. We can also witness the diminishing ego in the growing number of collaborative health care clinics, where professionals from different modalities work together under one roof.

Nevertheless, today's global health statistics show that a big change is still needed to occur for all health care practitioners to better serve all patients. A strong desire for positive action and results are needed, while financial motivations are a restriction that can be diminished. Finding and dedicating the time to learn can be restricted by financial desire and a need to serve the personal ego; to achieve status and prestige. Can you imagine a surgeon talking to a chiropractor? Do you think this has ever happened? Will it ever happen? We are here to say that it must!

The willingness to have an open mind; to communicate and to take the time to do so is needed. This is why this book is has been written: to stimulate all health care practitioners and patients to take more responsibility for their own wellbeing. Rather than being the obedient, patient dreamer, hoping for the doctor's magic or a magic pill, herb, machine, etc., the onus is on the patient to entice their health care practitioner to dig deep, all the way to the cause of disease. We need to find the necessary encouragement to enter the new health care horizon. Holistic integration of health care knowledge from all sources, ranging from the shaman to the Functional Medicine doctor and everything in between. We need it all.

To reach this new realm of health care understanding, each practitioner must be willing to take the initiative towards change. The patient must wake from a childish passivity into an adult sense of responsibility by being active in their health consultations. This means that health care practitioners must make time to answer questions and patiently listen to patient concerns.

When a patient prepares themself by studying their own diseased condition, they are asking questions and discussing their situation with the understanding necessary for a responsible dialogue between patient and practitioner. There is no need to simply obey all orders with little to no understanding. In fact, we would advise against any such practices! As Buddhism proposes, you *are* the power and have the responsibility, so there is no sense in blaming your environment.

Patients usually look to their chosen health care practitioner as an authority who knows and understands each of their health problems, and who also knows the solution. With this in mind, the patient enters the consultation and listens respectfully, perhaps even reverently, as has been learned in previous encounters with the health care industry. In my personal experience, I have found that most doctors, after hearing the presented problem, give little room for more information or questions from the patient. The doctor will listen to a patient's symptoms and take over from there, which tends to inhibit more patient information that can be helpful to diagnosis and treatment. This is the case with nearly all "insurance doctors" around the world, who are told to operate under limited time constraints. They are told to "produce" numbers in order to maintain their position. I have personally found non-insurance doctors to be more patient, allowing for more time in the consultation process.

Those doctors who are open to learning from both their patients and from other treatment modalities will find that it benefits their own professional knowledge and practice. Contrarily, a doctor who feels threatened by the gaps in their knowledge may deprive themself of all the gains that come from an interchange of disciplines. Not only does the close minded doctor hurt themself and their patients, they also do not get to experience the joy gained by enhancing their knowledge. The closed-minded doctor is missing a personal good feeling through experiencing personal and professional growth.

Integrative holistic team prevention, diagnosis and treatment has rewards in many areas. The patient, the doctor, individual budgets, government budgets, and the health of the environment all benefit. The patient benefits from better health when he learns about better living habits for daily life, building their knowledge from the ground up; from prevention to proper diagnosis and treatment. Individual needs and deficiencies must be addressed to contribute to better general health, like proper diet and sleep, regular exercise, positive thinking, control of emotional reactions and addressing spiritual concerns. Each of these facets of the human experience can have a significant impact on health.

Every health care practitioner will learn that they must go beyond the limits of their training and their possible financial greed. They must overcome the parts of their professional ego that block them from experiencing joy in their personal and professional growth. Through the growth of the aforementioned areas, the costs of treatment (financial and physical) and the duration of treatment can be reduced. The governments that fund public hospitals and health insurance will be able to reduce their public health care budgets. This may not be liked by the insurance and pharmaceutical companies that must create more profits for their stockholders.

When the patient learns about better dietary choices, such as choosing organic food over GMO, or food grown with large amounts of chemicals, or food filled with some of the over 10,000 food additives in processed foods, the environment benefits. When we take control of our diets and strive for clean air, water and mineral rich soil, the environment benefits. Bottled water often has nano particles of plastic floating in the water, which are harmful when consumed over time. Drinking more bottled water means more plastic ending up in our water sources. Ingesting plastic through heating, scratching or other micro particles is a known carcinogenic risk[4]. Learning about cause and reaction is the part that we can play in our own disease prevention. Putting all of the information together will be a benefit to humanity. It is up to all of us to take on the responsibility of educating ourselves alongside the growing information in all aspects relevant to our individual lives, with a special focus placed on our number one priority: our health.

---

[4] https://ntp.niehs.nih.gov/ntp/roc/content/listed_substances_508.pdf

Beyond these motivations for writing this book, my personal motivation includes the inadequate medical treatment that I have personally received. I have a chronic condition that I will live with for the rest of my life because of my own lack of knowledge and lack of questioning my health care practitioners. I believe that I experienced medical incompetence and negligence; however, ultimately, I now hold myself accountable for not doing more research on my own. We must ask the questions: Why do so many doctors not take on the responsibility of professional growth? And why do they not make the changes in themselves and their professional practices that will bring better health to all? Bottom lines are usually found in fear and laziness (not wanting to do the necessary work), so we should be safe to assume that these are two of the top reasons for why not. Most people want to be nourished and entertained after their day's work. Additional, unpaid "work" in the form of studying is not usually on the average person's (or doctor's) agenda.

Fear is typically unconscious in many people and change is difficult to address when a fear is unacknowledged. Various fears may be present, such as fearing for the safety of one's professional ego, self-esteem or social status. It is not a nice feeling to recognize that you don't in fact *know it all* and you probably never will. Even within the same profession, there may be a lack of communication between practitioners coming from different viewpoints and a hesitancy to make an intra-professional referral may develop. Deriving income from insurance-based sources may limit a doctor's ability to face themself because of their dependence on a much larger entity that doesn't have the time or resources for "further study." In a timed scenario, there is no place to look in the mirror and reflect with self-observation, much less self-evaluation, and no time to test paths that may lead to change. Regardless, we feel comfortable saying this with ease: staying comfortably where you are may actually be equivalent to floating backwards. As the world changes rapidly, this message is for everyone standing still: take responsibility for your health now. Do not avoid it and wait for another day. The world is moving ahead, with or without you.

To take responsibility, both motivation and discipline are required. To develop motivation, one must become aware of what choices are available.

For most of us, by developing great energy and vitality, we can avoid extreme pain, suffering, and premature aging. Most people wait for a crisis to motivate them, but change is best started today. Don't use defenses like the desire to procrastinate, avoid and deny. Become more disciplined by breaking down bad habits formed over many years. By starting as easy as you want and steadily increasing at your own rate, you will learn discipline successfully. But without converting knowledge into action, there will be no real progress. Change requires regular effort.

What Is Integrative Holistic Health Care?

The foundational purpose of this book is to show that each of the diagnostic and treatment modalities available to us offer their own element of health awareness and healing benefits. In fact, every modality in the world has at least a little something helpful that can be adapted and applied in coalition with other modalities to get a clearer picture of health and how to achieve it. All of the various traditional and contemporary modalities offer information that is worthwhile to the healing process, and when multiple modalities are "integrated," the whole of this database of knowledge becomes greater than the sum of its parts; open to the addition of new elements that will create a greater whole.

Independently, though, any modality is limited in its scope and needs to learn from other modalities to achieve an integrative holistic team approach. Health care practitioners need to cooperate with one another to truly be able to offer the best care to their patients. They need to have more open minds and to possibly make a small financial sacrifice.

We have the hope that, first and foremost, healing practitioners of any modality choose to enter into their professions in order to help people. Their idealistic goals as students may have been lost in the development of their professional egos (marketing their "brand", being paid by recommendations/referrals, etc), but they don't have to be lost forever. When the team approach is utilized, both patients and professionals will benefit by getting something back. The patient will benefit from a better understanding of their path to healing. The health care practitioner will get back their professional integrity, in keeping with the necessary desire to continue learning and studying in order to grow continually in their abilities. A team approach is the easiest way to achieve this and is, thus, the future of health care.

This team approach should be—and is—the future of health care.

***

The first goal of this book is to review some of the main modalities of healing practices, including diet and exercise regimes, with the goal of giving the health care practitioner a clearer picture of what is currently available for patients, along with some effort given to offering the strengths and weaknesses of each of these carefully selected modalities, as determined by our team of fallible authors. We have selected the modalities that we believe to be most notably representative of the wide variety of available modalities of healing on offer today. They are by no means representative of what we believe to be the best options for diagnosis, treatment or prevention. The point is that it's up to all of us, as patients and practitioners, to learn and decide for ourselves.

The second goal is to teach patients and practitioners how to evaluate and integrate what is useful in their patients' and their own healing processes.

The third goal is to facilitate the communication between any and all practitioners of health care in a non-competitive way that is conducive to learning from one another.

The ultimate goal is to apply all of this knowledge into every patient's treatment and healing process, and to help practitioners and patients in the most effective way for all involved.

We need a system of intra-professional communication, where heart specialists talk to urologists, not just send their patients for referrals. And we need there to be a system of inter-professional communication, where psychologists talk to medical doctors. If this doesn't happen, a great deficit will continue to occur in the patient's care

And so, can the doctor's heart, mind, and intuition combine with technology and money in a creative and helpful way? We sincerely hope so, because eventually, even a doctor will get sick and have a crisis for which they will need good care. Waking up now is a personal gain for any doctor considering their own future health care.

What Is The Goal Of Holistic Health Care?

Ayurveda, which is thought to be one of the oldest forms of medicine, dates back 2,500 years. It is said to contain 35,000 remedies for various illnesses. The theory of Ayurveda is predicated on a belief that the human body contains an individual balance of three forces in human equilibrium, called *doshas*.

In 2,600 BC, the Egyptian Pharaoh Imhotep described the diagnoses of 200 diseases in hieroglyph.

Hippocrates, born in 460 BC, began the tradition of the scientific study of medicine.

Traditional Chinese Medicine dates back to 2,500 BC and is founded on a belief that vital energy (called *chi* or *Qi*) circulates through channels in the body that are connected to the body's organs and their functions.

Each of these examples of alternative healing systems use products and practices that are not a part of the traditional scope of western medicine. Many of their individual tenets conflict with one another, but many core ideas are consistent between them.

Western medicine is a system in which medical doctors, nurses, pharmacists and therapists treat symptoms and diseases using drugs, radiation, chemotherapy and surgery. Western medicine is scientifically known as allopathic medicine. It is meant to be the method of treating disease by the use of agents that produce effects different from those of the disease treated (as opposed to homeopathy, which uses the same agent in different doses to change the effect—whether it accomplishes this purpose is up for debate). In allopathic medicine, the primary methods of treatment are drugs and surgery. The allopathic system of medicine had many discoveries in the last two centuries, including anaesthesia (1846), germ theory (1861), medical imaging (1895), Penicillin (1928), how to perform organ transplants (1954), stem cell therapy (1970s), immunotherapy (1970s), and recent advances like learning how to disarm HIV (2018). The types of advances in emergency care have resulted in allopathic becoming the prevailing system of healing, also known as "modern medicine."

Holistic medicine is different to the many individual traditions of alternative and allopathic healing systems. Holistic theory has four basic principles:

1. People have an innate healing power.
2. The patient is a person, not a disease.
3. Healing needs a team approach that involves the patient and doctor jointly addressing all aspects of a person's life.
4. Treatment involves addressing the cause and not only alleviating the symptom.

Holistic theory also states that love and support are powerful healers, and that people are responsible for their own health. It is the most logical evolution of medicine that takes into account the core values of love for self and others, compassion, integrity and respect. It requires the professional cooperation of different practitioners and their enthusiasm to meet in a team approach to discuss a patient's diagnosis and treatment with significant involvement from the patient.

It is unlikely that a typical patient can afford to pay for a team diagnosis and treatment plan, and so, until now, holistic healing has not been in the scope of general knowledge or possibility. But we are undeterred by the lack of precedence in the field of holistic therapy because patients are growing in intelligence and asking that their chosen healers, from any modality, have open minds; to be willing to devote a portion of their energy to a more comprehensive understanding of a patient's ailments, thus creating and cultivating the most efficient and effective path to healing.

My personal definition of holistic health care is that it is the integration of an ever expanding field of knowledge. This integration involves learning of the interdependence between the interactive parts of prevention, evaluation, diagnosis and treatment, aimed at combining all aspects of symptoms and causes of disease. To achieve this, a combination of all available information from all health care modalities is needed. It is essential to have awareness of all aspects of a person's physical, mental, emotional and spiritual life, continually opening to new investigations and findings in the ever expanding and changing fields of personal and collective nutrition, energy and microbiome. Holistic health care must remain in an open frame, in which all new, verifiably-studied information is reinvested into the system, with no room for any fixed belief system.

Why Is Now The Time To Pursue This Goal?

When the ego gets in the way of truth, truth remains undiscovered.
When the ego says, I am right, it closes the door of the discovery of new information.

Our outdated beliefs stand in the way of our progress. They are, however, often defended for the sake of our egos. But new information is a threat to more than just the ego. It can also be a threat to the financial systems built on old beliefs, once thought to be solid as stone. The primary goal of health care should be to help the patient. The primary goal of health care should not be to confirm the training and beliefs of the practitioner, or the creation of an empire of wealth and/or knowledge.

The now universally-recognized image of a smiling alternative doctor differs greatly from the one we have known; who stares at the computer, typing with two fingers as they interview their patient. The insurance doctor who has been restricted to a fifteen minute meeting has quotas to meet, rather than reserving more time for patients and gathering information. The patient is merely an engine to generate income for the insurance company, more so than a person to be helped. These are no longer the days that a doctor comes to your home carrying his little black bag, ready to help by whatever means they possess.

The doctor's tone of voice, body language and genuine concern are all a part of the art of healing. It is time for us to remember and appreciate that the unspoken emotions and the true motivation of the doctor are, on some level, perceived by the patient. A doctor's personal history is embedded in their cells and written on their face. They are best prepared to treat when they have taken the time to resolve as many of their own personal issues as possible. Psychoanalytic training, for instance, requires the student to have intensive sessions of personal psychoanalysis. This is not always feasible or required within other professions. This book, however, does contain a list of suggested requirements that we feel should be considered as part of any health care professional's training.

Upon graduating, most doctors seek jobs straight away, largely in part to pay for their massive school debts. The most available jobs for fresh graduates are within the medical insurance industry, which pays a more steady wage than starting one's own practice. But as we mentioned before, it also comes with time and referral pressures. I have had the experience of witnessing a doctor become angry when I asked a detailed question when they did not know the answer. "I don't know" can be a helpful enough answer in ascertaining the next step; more so than a confident but baseless answer.

An educated patient can come out of the conditioned role of helplessness and become an active participant in their health care. Just having the option to learn will give a patient the regained sense of strength that they need to begin their recovery process. The passive victim is less likely to recover than the active helper-type patient, who wants to aid in their own recovery and future prevention process.

The vast majority of health care patients today have been trained by society, culture and industry to listen to the doctor about health in the same way that we listen to the mechanic about car problems. Most of us are lay people when it comes to car mechanics and we trust the "experts" to diagnose and fix our car problems. And we do the same with our bodily mechanics, too. Most of us lack the foundational knowledge to understand how to prevent disease, let alone how to treat it. It is time that we all learn how to check our bodily "gages" to see if they "light up" when we test them. It is understandable that when you go to the doctor, you may be a bit anxious about your pain and therefore prone to obey quickly out of fear for your health. But really, why not ask the doctor about the cause of your pain?

The most effective healing process is when the body, mind and spirit work together. Treating a symptom is not healing and we must never forget that the body heals itself. No doctor in the world can heal a cut-the body does it.

"We are what we repeatedly do. Excellence, then, is not an act, but a habit." —Aristotle

Prevention Vs. Crisis

I have now come to accept that even the most intelligent people will wait for a health crisis rather than do what is necessary to prevent a crisis. Most people are consistently partially ill but their symptoms do not bother them enough to evaluate their own health situation internally. They tend to rationalize their abdominal fat, protruding belly, stress, negative emotions and conflicts by using the typical 'health scapegoats,' like blaming environment, hormones, or simply having a good time. The emotional issues that prevent people from being objective often serve as a good defense against exposing themselves to information based on scientific study or even rare moments of personal reflection. Denial is a defense used commonly by many people who deal with health issues.

The amount of scientific studies and research that is available to the public from reputable sources is enormous and it's increasing all of the time. Despite this bloom in publicly available resources, some of the most intelligent people in the world, like medical doctors, have refused to look at the information, even when presented to them. I will never forget the story of a doctor I was working with in New York when I was working for large health insurance provider. This doctor had to have a triple bypass before he was ready to listen to me about the foods he was eating.

If you are having any type of minor health problem, whether it is physical, mental or emotional, it makes sense to investigate it before it gets worse. If you keep living the lifestyle that you have been living up to now, chances are good that the problems will continue to persist and possibly grow. Open your mind to prevention—don't wait for the crisis.

Attitude Is Important

As you read this book you may be asking yourself: *what is my attitude towards my health?*

The term 'attitude' has many meanings:

- Your thoughts, feelings, values, beliefs, emotions and actions
- A mental position, disposition, position, orientation of the mind
- Positive or negative, conscious or unconscious, a way of responding to things
- Cool, cocky, defiant, arrogant, accepting, open minded

The information in this book can add new health to your life when you look at your attitude as you read: the more open you are, the better you can understand the information herein.

Integrative Prevention Team Diagnosis

Understanding the precursors and early signs of disease can help prevent an illness from developing. These early signs can be discovered and used to prevent a symptom or symptoms from developing. Traditionally, though, a disease is treated only when a symptom shows itself. With the tools for understanding health now available, there is no longer a need to get sick and suffer in order to treat symptoms. The current emphasis on locating the cause of the symptom is becoming more accepted and used in modern practice.

Finding the early signs or precursors can best be achieved by using an Integrative Prevention Team Diagnosis (IPTD). This refers to a patient soliciting the knowledge and resources of a variety of disciplines, taking place in a central location where the findings of each discipline can be presented, discussed and coordinated as a team. A tentative conclusion can be reached and presented in a skillful manner to the patient so that a decision to take action for a change in lifestyle by the patient can be made. For example, the team members may include an iridologist, a live blood cell analyst, a medical doctor reviewing homocysteine, triglycerides, cholesterol, etc., a nutritionist, a massage therapist, a chiropractor, a psychotherapist, an herbalist, a naturopath, a natural hygienist, an acupuncturist, and so on. The essence is to capture as many perspectives and as many skill sets into one Integrative Prevention Team Diagnosis. The findings from these professional disciplines will be presented at a team meeting in which the goal will be to fully understand, discuss, coordinate and conclude how best to help the patient from developing a disease. This team prevention diagnostic approach shall always be the main focus. There is no room in this team for professionals to become sidetracked by their personal agendas, egos or ideas of professional hierarchies. Skillful leadership of this team will facilitate and enable teamwork to be utilized, with full respect to each member.

To initiate IPTD, the team members will need to commit time every week to building rapport within the team, without remuneration (at least initially). This will primarily be an experimental, heartfelt and loving process, which will be motivated by truth and a desire to help prevent needless human suffering. The success of this new model will depend on the team members willingness and motivation to commit to this cause. The development of prototype wellness centers that feature a number of different alternative disciplines has served as the basis for future of health care, with more well-rounded centers that include mainstream allopathic practitioners and holistic healing professionals.

The far reaching consequences of such a system of disease prevention will decrease human suffering, premature deaths, help the ecology of the planet and save trillions of dollars spent on current health care practices.

Opposition to an IPTD model may arise from those who currently benefit financially from the status quo. However, if they want to help their own children, families and themselves, they would be wise to see the benefits in such an approach. The development and rise of illnesses and new diseases, such as childhood cancer and diabetes, despite new technologies and medical equipment, points to the need for early detection and prevention. Let us carry forth this plan with courage, love, enthusiasm, dedication, persistence and commitment.

Wake Up, World

Every day your health, your energy, your money, your life, and your children's lives are being destroyed. The air you breathe, the food you eat, and the water you drink are making you sick and robbing you of your vitality, slowly creating pain, suffering, and premature death. Those of us who have built our lives around studying such matters are aware of what is happening to the planet and ourselves and we want to help. And truly, everything starts with us. We can change ourselves; no one else can change us. We can present a challenge to ourselves and to the world, because without a challenge, there can be no change. If we change the way we think, we can start to change our lifestyles. If we wait for a crisis in our lives to motivate us, we deprive ourselves of a head start toward preventing disease. Collectively and individually, we create our own challenges.

When we weaken our immune systems, we become more vulnerable to the invasion of microbes and viruses that were already there. And when we give our bodies, minds, and spirits the proper "food," nourishment takes place. Every cell in our bodies pulsates seventy times a minute, needing the right nutrients to continue pulsating and eliminating wastes. If this does not occur properly, the cell weakens and becomes diseased. As the diseased cells build up over time, a blockage occurs and a disease slowly forms, which calls our attention in the form of a symptom. When the symptom becomes annoying enough or painful enough, we seek relief.

We must wake up now or suffer the consequences of what the powers that be are doing to our air, water, food, and to us. These powers are destroying our planet in exchange for money from the corporations that they control. Their actions have resulted in, among other things, an epidemic of children with "old-people's" diseases such as cancer, diabetes, and arthritis. Additionally, many new "diseases" like Attention Deficit and Hyperactivity Disorder (A.D.H.D.) or restless leg syndrome are being exploited in order to sell new drugs. In the case of A.D.H.D., Dr. Keith Connors, who led the fight to legitimize the disorder, admits that 10% of the 15% of diagnoses are incorrect, calling them "a national disaster of dangerous proportions."[5] He goes so far as to say that the excessive diagnoses are "a concoction to justify the giving out of medication at unprecedented and unjustifiable levels."

In a 2013 article called *The Selling of Attention Deficit Disorder,* the New York Times published that the rise of A.D.H.D. diagnoses and prescriptions for stimulants over the years "coincided with a remarkably successful two-decade campaign by pharmaceutical companies to publicize the syndrome and promote the pills to doctors, educators and parents. With the children's market booming, the industry is now employing similar marketing techniques as it focuses on adult A.D.H.D., which could become even more profitable."[6] Even the pharmaceutical executive who introduced Adderall in 1994, Roger Griggs, said he strongly opposes marketing stimulants to the general public because of their dangers, calling them "nuclear bombs" and their usage should be overseen by health care professionals.[7] With about 7,000 prescription drugs available on the US market and a host of new medical devices, diseases are still on the rise!

---

[5] https://www.nytimes.com/2013/12/15/health/the-selling-of-attention-deficit-disorder.html

[6] https://www.nytimes.com/2013/12/15/health/the-selling-of-attention-deficit-disorder.html

[7] https://www.nytimes.com/2013/12/15/health/the-selling-of-attention-deficit-disorder.html

As more people turn to alternatives to the mainstream disease-care system, pharmaceutical companies are inventing new drugs for children to "prevent" illness. You won't have to look far in order to verify this. So why give a healthy child toxic drugs to prevent a disease he does not have? This insane thinking is motivated by profit at the expense of the health and lives of our children. The propaganda machine brainwashes the unsuspecting, uninformed population. Promoting disease is also the business of the baby food industry. Recent laboratory tests of eight industry-leader baby foods revealed the presence of 16 pesticides, including three carcinogens[8]. Processed and cooked baby foods also lack the full complement of vital nutrients, including enzymes, that are found in whole foods in their natural state. Such "dead" enzyme-deficient foods line the shelves of all supermarkets and many health-food stores.

It is our opinion that many corporations are motivated by financial interests to invent diseases, such as 'restless leg syndrome,' to sell new drugs. The weakening of organic farm standards and the financial contributions of a major fast food chain to one of the most prestigious medical schools in the United States are two examples of this corporate corruption. There are many corporations, such as Proctor and Gamble, Philip Morris, Coca Cola, Archer Daniels Midland, and so on, that contribute to disease such as childhood cancer and diabetes.[9]

The powers that be refuse to open their ears and minds because obtaining and maintaining control and money are more seductive goals than providing the tools for good health for the general populace. The powerful have the money to overwhelm our better sense with sensationalistic media. Count the number of drug commercials that you see on TV in one day! Clearly, the goal of these irresponsible and self-serving advertisements is to keep people coming back for more, and not to enhance their health. There are commercials for reducing heart disease or alleviating gastric pains that don't say anything about eating better or leading a less stressful life.

[8] Levine, Marvin J. Pesticides: A Toxic Time Bomb in Our Midst. Greenwood Publishing Company, 2007.
[9] Avoidable Causes of Childhood Cancer, By Samuel S. Epstein, MD

The powers that be are also hard at work, endeavoring to weaken global standards for organic certification of our foods and other products. If the global food markets continue in their current trends, high-quality, organically grown food will soon be very hard to find, and processed foods and genetically modified foods, which contain more than 10,000 additives, will continue to increase on store shelves. Transnational conglomerates are often successful at lobbying national governments and their food and drug administrations. Monsanto, for instance, is patenting and thereby taking control of the global seed market.[10]

It's time that we educate ourselves and develop a grass-roots movement that grows strong enough to have a voice that will wake us up; to become a vibrant, healthy people, led by truth, dignity, and enthusiasm. Get your family and friends to spread the word, and be sure to include your children. When we all become leaders in our personal spheres, we will save ourselves and the planet. Small steps combine to create giant leaps!

The health care industries around the world depend on illness to survive financially. How can they get paid if they don't see you? When you are well, you do not need their services. If you are healthy, you may never be a patient unless you have an accident.

Catalyzing Global Change

The evolution of global consciousness is growing, as shown by the formation of groups strongly committed to creating positive change. Those upholding truth, love and sanity are facing insane, corrupt, greedy killers who lack personal integrity. These greed-filled entities are intent on destroying people and the planet for their short-term, selfish gains. Their illusions of control and power cannot succeed, since they are self-destructive, shortsighted, and on the side of fear rather than love. They are the system that we continue to rebel against. We use love to mobilize into

---

[10] https://www.organicconsumers.org/news/seeds-evil-monsanto-and-genetic-engineering

action; to come out of our passive, helpless, hopeless state. We are waking up and finally taking action.

So what can you do to start? Begin by taking care of yourself and your family, by making responsible choices and evaluating the consequences of those choices. We can help ourselves and each other by becoming part of this evolution that is leading to spiritual growth, love, peace and fellowship. We are all part of nature and not separate from the natural world. We are part of each other and must not become separated by different beliefs. When we practice being peaceful and loving every day, remembering and communicating in the international language of a smile, we are doing our part to move in the direction that is crucial to our continuance as a species.

I hope this makes you think about change, which can only come when you start to make changes in your life. You have the power, so use it the best way you can. Accept your personal challenges with enthusiasm and love. Have the courage to change how you think, believe, feel and act. Start today, because you and your children are the seeds of the future.

PART 2:

Modern Medicine And The Alternatives

"Health is the greatest possession. Contentment is the greatest treasure. Confidence is the greatest friend. Non-being is the greatest joy." - Lao Tzu

A SELECTION OF MODALITIES

We have chosen the following list of modalities to be a small representation of the sum total of health care modalities available to the modern patient. We have chosen these modalities for no scientific reason. Rather, we chose the modalities that we understand to have the largest followings in their respective health care communities.

Allopathic medicine is the obvious "benchmark" to which our modern global expectations for health care is set. We have chosen three specifically Eastern modalities—Reiki, Ayurveda and Traditional Chinese Medicine—to give ourselves and our readers an understanding of how the traditional Eastern vision of health care differs from traditional Western modalities, like Chiropractic or Osteopathy. We do not claim to be offering a completely "whole-istic" picture of all that modern health care has to offer, but we do feel that it is a good sampling of what types of modalities are available, built around a narrative of where they originate from, why they developed how they did, and where they stand within the mainstream health care community and its alternative counterparts.

Conventional Allopathic Medicine

According to the book The Future of Medicine: Megatrends in Healthcare That Will Improve Your Quality of Life by Stephen C. Schimpff, the future of health care is in technology and more machines for diagnoses and treatments. These health care machines will provide examinations and blood analysis, which we tend to view as reliable results. Generally speaking, though, the trend of technology shows that it is eating away at our humanity, detaching us from any results that we receive. Technology both helps and harms, as evidenced by the example of smartphones, which help us communicate more easily while also irradiating and monitoring users continuously.

Allopathic health care is compartmentalized. It tends to ignore the inter-relationships between our body parts, mind, thoughts, and emotions. Allopathic doctors generally prescribe medications for symptom relief and make referrals for tests, procedures and surgeries. Symptom relief is preferred by allopathic medicine because it is quick and profitable. MRIs have become a good business. Cancer has become a major industry. Sick, frightened, suffering, anxious and unaware patients do what they are told by doctors. Even the allopathic doctors believe what they are practicing in their professions and many don't know the truth about what the alternative modalities have to offer.

"It is simply no longer possible to believe much of the clinical research that is published, or to rely on the judgment of trusted physicians or authoritative medical guidelines. I take no pleasure in this conclusion, which I reached slowly and reluctantly over my two decades as an editor of The New England Journal of Medicine." —Marcia Angell, MD

Thanks to the meticulous reporting by medical researchers like Jon Rappoport, we know that doctors, medical schools, medical journals, mainstream medical reporters, drug companies, and the FDA all rely on published clinical trials of drugs to determine whether they are safe and effective to prescribe and publicize. Without these studies, the whole field of medical research would fall apart in utter chaos. Doctors are expected to have read the published reports in the medical journals that describe the clinical trials. Or if the doctors haven't actually read the reports, they've been told about them. Nevertheless, according to the New York Review of Books (May 12, 2011) by Helen Epstein, *Flu Warning: Beware the Drug Companies*:

"Six years ago, John Ioannidis, a professor of epidemiology at the University of Ioannina School of Medicine in Greece, found that nearly half of published articles in scientific journals contained findings that were false, in the sense that independent researchers couldn't replicate them. The problem is particularly widespread in medical research, where peer-reviewed articles in medical journals can be crucial in influencing multimillion- and sometimes multibillion-dollar spending decisions. It would be surprising if conflicts of interest did not sometimes compromise editorial neutrality, and in the case of medical research, the sources of bias are obvious. Most medical journals receive half or more of their income from pharmaceutical company advertising and reprint orders, and dozens of others [journals] are owned by companies like Wolters Kluwer, a medical publisher that also provides marketing services to the pharmaceutical industry.

"...The FDA also relies increasingly upon fees and other payments from the pharmaceutical companies whose products the agency is supposed to regulate. This could contribute to the growing number of scandals in which the dangers of widely prescribed drugs have been discovered too late. Last year, GlaxoSmithKline's diabetes drug Avandia was linked to thousands of heart attacks, and earlier in the decade, the company's antidepressant Paxil was discovered to exacerbate the risk of suicide in young people[11]. Merck's painkiller Vioxx was also linked to thousands of heart disease deaths. In each case, the scientific literature gave little hint of these dangers. The companies have agreed to pay settlements in class action lawsuits amounting to far less than the profits the drugs earned on the market. These precedents could be creating incentives for reduced vigilance concerning the side effects of prescription drugs in general."

Also from the NY Review of Books is an article titled "Drug Companies and Doctors: A Story of Corruption" by Marcia Angell, former editor-in-chief of The New England Journal of Medicine, which is perhaps the most prestigious medical journal in the world. Here's a short excerpt explaining her view on sponsored trials:

"Consider the clinical trials by which drugs are tested in human subjects. Before a new drug can enter the market, its manufacturer must sponsor clinical trials to show the Food and Drug Administration that the drug is safe and effective, usually as compared with a placebo or dummy pill. The results of all the trials (there may be many) are submitted to the FDA, and if

---

[11]   https://www.nytimes.com/2010/02/20/health/policy/20avandia.html

one or two trials are positive-that is, they show effectiveness without serious risk-the drug is usually approved, even if all the other trials are negative.

"...In view of this control and the conflicts of interest that permeate the enterprise, it is not surprising that [drug] industry-sponsored trials published in medical journals consistently favor sponsors' drugs-largely because negative results are not published, positive results are repeated in slightly different forms, and a positive spin is put on even negative results. A review of seventy-four clinical trials of antidepressants, for example, found that thirty-seven of thirty-eight positive studies were published. But of the thirty-six negative studies, thirty-three were either not published or published in a form that conveyed a positive outcome."

Dr. Barbara Starfield's famous study, *Is US health really the best in the world?*, from the Journal of the American Medical Association, July 26, 2000 concludes that 225,000 people are killed by the medical system in the US every year, and 106,000 by FDA-approved medicines. This latter figure works out to over one million deaths per decade. But as doctors in the west become more aware of other cultural practices, especially from the ancient eastern cultures and from indigenous peoples around the world, they begin to realize that there is a wealth of information about disease and its various causes and treatments that goes beyond what allopathic medicine offers its patients.

Allopathic doctors need to be a part of the integrative health care process. As students, they did not know what they were getting into and were brainwashed about the medical profession and their education by the drug companies. Many of them are now changing over by moving in the direction of plant-based diet. Some allopathic practitioners, like Dr. Neil Bernhard, have seen the problems with generally accepted allopathic practices. But it is the practitioners who are caught in a desire for building money and ego who need help. They need help to break away from their ties to pharmaceutical companies and from the limited thinking promoted by insurance companies. Once they recognize that the body heals itself, they will break out of the existing allopathic system and into the integrative health care process. Those practitioners who choose to go into the allopathic system are usually unaware that their education is largely controlled by drug companies and their own findings. They have been brainwashed about their role in becoming a doctor. They may be good people with good intentions but they are lacking in awareness of the negative aspects regarding allopathic diagnosis and treatment of disease. The body heals itself with proper nutrition, exercise, sleep, thinking and environment, as well as the elimination of toxins in our physical, mental, emotional and spiritual realms.

Historical/Resurgence Modalities

"Change yourself and you have done your part in changing the world."
—Paramhansa Yogananda

Hailing from the ancient eastern traditions of China, India, and Japan, Traditional Chinese Medicine, Ayurveda and Reiki all have long histories that lead into their current healing theories. Even Reiki, the newest of the three, stems from philosophical traditions created by ancient masters. Each of these modalities works to understand the core of the patient's issue by looking down the path that took the patient to disease. If we should take anything from the some of the earth's oldest living cultures, it is the idea that if we want to learn of our future, it is best to look at our past.

Traditional Chinese Medicine

"A Profound Pathway to Health"

History

Traditional Chinese medicine (TCM for short) is a healing modality built on a foundation of more than 2500 years of Chinese medical practice. This history includes various forms of herbal medicine, acupuncture, massage, exercise (qigong), and nutritional therapy. The doctrines of TCM are rooted in Chinese canonic literature, as well as in cosmological theories such as *yin-yang* (the theory of how seemingly opposite forces may actually be complementary) and the five elements (water, earth, air, fire, and metal).

TCM is widely used throughout Greater China as the standard system of medicine, and is becoming increasingly recognized worldwide as an alternative form of medicine. It has recently been influenced by modern Western medicine and in the 1950s, the Chinese government promoted a systematized form of TCM, integrating the precepts with modern notions of anatomy and pathology.

Theory

A basic tenet of TCM is that the body's vital energy, known as Chi, circulates through channels in the body, called meridians. These meridians are connected to bodily organs and functions, giving indication if there is something wrong with the organs and their functions. It emphasizes the dynamic processes of the body over the material structure thereof.

Chi is defined by five cardinal functions:

1. Actuation of the physical processes of the body
2. Warming of the body, especially of the limbs
3. Defense against external factors
4. Containment of bodily fluids from excessive emission
5. Transformation of intake (food, drink, breath, parental influence/genetics) into Chi, blood and fluids

In TCM, the concepts of yin and yang is applied to the human body. The upper part of the body (including the back) are assigned to yang, and the lower part of the body is assigned to yin. This concept extends to the various bodily functions.

The yin and yang of the body are seen as phenomena whose lack or over-abundance comes with characteristic symptom combinations:

- Yin vacuity results in heat sensations, sweating at night, insomnia, dry pharynx, dry mouth, dark urine and a rapid pulse.
- Yang vacuity results in an aversion to cold, cold limbs, bright, white complexion, long voidings of clear urine, diarrhea, pale and enlarged tongue, and a weak, slow pulse.

The *Five Phases* theory of TCM presumes that all phenomena of nature can be broken down into five elemental qualities. Strict rules are identified to apply to the relationship between the five elements, including the sequence of the elements, how they act on one another, and so on. There are five yin elemental organs, and five yang elemental organs defined in TCM.

Practice

Diagnosis aims to trace symptoms to patterns of an underlying disharmony in the body. Practitioners measure the patient's pulse, inspect the tongue, skin, and eyes, and ask questions about the eating and sleeping habits of the patient. TCM's view of the human body is only marginally concerned with anatomical structures. It focuses primarily on the body's functions, such as digestion, breathing, temperature maintenance, etc. These functions are associated with a primary functional entity that dictates that function.

In TCM, disease is perceived as a disharmony in the interaction between the human body and the environment. Understanding and discerning the patterns of harmony is known to be the most difficult aspect of practicing TCM. To determine which pattern is in effect, practitioners will examine the patient for markers of imbalance, such as the color of the tongue, or the strength of pulse-points. According to TCM, disease has two aspects: the diagnosis and the syndrome. Although the diagnosis may be the same in two patients, the syndrome can differ (and vice versa). Therapy is chosen based on the patients syndrome (also known as the "pattern"). This means that patients with different diseases may receive the same treatment because their disease pattern is the same.

The eight principles of defining syndromes in TCM are:

1. Yin
2. Yang
3. Exterior of the body
4. Interior of the body
5. Cold aversion
6. Heat aversion
7. Deficiency
8. Excess

The evaluation of these signs and symptoms is conducted by analyzing the body's meridians, qi, blood, fluids, and genetics.

TCM does not strongly differentiate between cause and effect, although there are three fundamental categories of disease causes: external (excesses), internal (emotions), and non-external-non-internal (diet, fatigue, sexual intemperance, trauma, and parasites).

The five methods of diagnosing disease in TCM are:

1. Inspection of physical markers on/in the face

2. Listening for particular sounds from the body
3. Perceiving bodily odors
4. Asking questions about the body's processes
5. Testing for palpitation

Traditional Therapies

Therapy in TCM is based on which pattern of disharmony is identified, and based on the preferences of the practitioner when it comes to choosing diagnostics and treatments.

Acupuncture is the most common TCM therapy. It is the insertion of needles into the skin, subcutaneous tissue, and muscles, typically at acupoints. Acupuncture is generally performed in conjunction with moxibustion, which involves burning mugwort on or near the skin at an acupoint. It is most often used for the relief of pain, but can be used for a wide range of conditions. In electro-acupuncture, an electric current is applied to the needles after insertion in order to further stimulate acupoints. TCM is generally used in combination with other forms of treatment. The human body also contains 365 acupoints spanning across the whole and corresponding with the number of days in the year. The number of main meridians is 12, corresponding with the number of rivers flowing through the ancient Chinese empire.

"Herbal medicine" (also known as medicinals) in TCM refers to botanic and non-botanic substances (animal, human and mineral products) being used in healing. There are roughly 13,000 medicinals and over 100,000 recipes recorded. Plant elements and extracts are the most common elements used, with non-botanics making up a very small percentage of prescribed medicinals. Other TCM therapies include massage, Qigong regulated breathing exercise, cupping, abrading the skin, nutritional therapy, and bone setting (for the treatment of trauma and injury).

In Modern Health Care

Modern studies of TCM have found that results from treatments are inconsistent, suggesting false positive results. Scientific investigation has found no evidence of Chi or meridians in the microbiology of human cells, but proponents of TCM claim that modern scientific research has so far missed the suspected interactions between various ingredients and the human body's complex biological systems. There is, however, disagreement between TCM practitioners on what diagnosis and treatments should be used for any given patient. Modern research continues to state that effectiveness of TCM herbal medicine is poorly researched and documented.

There are concerns over a number of potentially toxic, rare, or endangered plant and animal species that are used by TCM practitioners, including concerns over illegal trade and transport. Pharmaceutical research has explored the potential for the creation of new drugs from TCM traditional remedies, showing few successful results. Nature Magazine described TCM as a pseudoscience in which the majority of its treatments have no logical mechanism of action (the interaction between the body's receptors and the chemicals being implemented are not proven). TCM has been the subject of controversy in China in recent times, with arguments that it is a pseudoscience that should be abolished in the public health care system and in academia. In 2006, Chinese scholar Zhang Gongyao triggered a national debate with his article, entitled Farewell to Traditional Chinese Medicine, arguing this point. However, the Chinese government took the stance that TCM is a science and continued to encourage its development in favor of continuing export revenues from TCM products. Despite the above listed controversies, most governments around the world have enacted laws to regulate the practice of TCM. In the US, only six states do not have existing regulation for the practice of TCM, meaning that clinics and practitioners are well-regulated in a large part of the western world.

Ayurveda

"Life Knowledge from the Gods"

History

Ayurveda is an ancient system of medicine originating in the Indian subcontinent. It can be traced back 2500 years and is thought to have originated from the Gods. One of the first and most powerful mind-body health systems, it calls itself a 'science of life' (Ayur = life, and Veda = science/knowledge).

Theory

The practice of Ayurveda is proposed to do more than simply treat illness. It offers ancient and sophisticated knowledge for health and vitality.

Two main principles of Ayurveda are:

1. The mind and the body are indivisible
2. The mind is the most powerful tool for transforming and healing the body

It is believed in Ayurveda that we gain freedom from illness by expanding our awareness in our mind; and through meditation, we bring this awareness into balance with our body. Restful awareness is also known as meditation, which is the practice of slowing heart rate through slowing breath. This practice decreases the stress hormones cortisol and adrenaline, and increases the wellbeing neurotransmitters serotonin, dopamine, oxytocin and endorphins.

Practice

Ayurveda is a personalized approach to health. Understanding unique mind-body types informs the practitioner's choices about diet, exercise, supplements, and personal care. Fresh foods should be appropriately prepared and eaten with awareness, according to Ayurveda. The simplest way to ensure you are eating a balanced diet is to include the six Ayurvedic tastes (sweet, salty, sour, bitter, pungent and astringent) in each meal. Filling your place with color is another method for a healthy diet. The body rejuvenates itself during natural, restful sleep, and a lack of restful sleep disrupts the mind-body balance. If one wakes up tired and non-energetic, sleep was not restful.

Ayurveda is about living in harmony with nature, including having healthy desires that match needs. Practitioners aim to flow in harmony with their bodily rhythms, such as sleeping, eating and experiencing sensations. Being out of rhythm means that desires become non-nurturing, resulting in indulgent and compulsive behaviors. Disorder breeds disease, which breeds stress and neglect, which causes more disorder. Exercise is used to tune into the body's messages, which are expressed through signals of comfort and discomfort. The mind lives in the past and the future, whereas the body lives in the now and asserts its needs with conviction. Awareness is achieved by asking the body how it feels about a decision and listening for messages of eagerness or distress.

Digestive energy, known as Agni (fire), should be strong, resulting in healthy tissues and the power to eliminate waste products efficiently. Strong digestive energy creates Ojas, which is a subtle essence thought to be the source of our vitality. Toxic residue, known as Ama, happens when digestive fire is weak, obstructing the flow of energy and immunity. There is no need for struggle in this approach, which is focused on simply aligning with nature. Motivating actions by love is the easiest way to align with nature, and chasing after status is a waste of energy.

Traditional Therapies

Therapies for mind-body imbalance include complex herbal compounds, minerals, metal substances, and some surgical techniques. Ayurveda describes three elemental substances called *Doshas* (humors), which are *Vata* (wind), *Pitta* (bile) and *Kapha* (phlegm). Equality of the doshas results in health and inequality in disease. Diagnosis is achieved through an eight-pronged approach of testing the pulse, urine, stool, tongue, speech, touch, vision and appearance. These factors are analyzed by a *guru* (teacher or guide) using their five senses.

In Modern Health Care

Modern science is only beginning to provide evidence for the mind-body connection that has been purported for millennia by Ayurvedic practitioners. The World Health Organization has recently established a traditional health care strategy (in 2002, and again in 2014), which incorporates Ayurveda.[12] This strategy suggests that its practices should be integrated into the overall health service delivery because it incorporates a personalized diet theory.

Health care industries today are experimenting with some Ayurvedic techniques in the laboratory, although no evidence has been found to date of its effectiveness for the treatment of any disease in particular. It is still considered a pseudoscience, and recent studies have found Indian-manufactured, patented Ayurvedic medicines to contain toxic levels of lead, mercury and arsenic.

Ayurveda does not offer echocardiograms or many other modern examinations and is therefore insufficient for diagnosing various forms of heart disease. It is ill-advised to treat heart patients without the use of echo-imaging to see the whole of the problem.

Reiki

"Life Force Energy Attunement"

Reiki and reflexology are two therapeutic modalities that are often utilized by the same practitioners of healing touch techniques for stress reduction and relaxation. For the purposes of being succinct, we will only expand upon Reiki, which precedes the practice of reflexology (healing touch aligned with pressure points on the feet and hands).

History

The secret art of inviting happiness
The miraculous medicine of all diseases
Just for today, do not anger
Do not worry and be filled with gratitude
Devote yourself to your work. Be kind to people.
Every morning and evening, join your hands in prayer.

---

[12] http://apps.who.int/gb/archive/pdf_files/WHA56/ea5618.pdf

Pray these words to your heart
and chant these words with your mouth

—Usui Reiki Treatment for the improvement of body and mind by the founder, Usui Mikao

The term 'Reiki' comes from the Japanese words *Rei* (meaning God's Wisdom or the Higher Power) and *Ki* (meaning life force energy). Together, they equal the definition: "spiritually guided life force energy."

Developed in 1922 by Japanese Buddhist, Dr. Mikao Usui, Reiki's ideals are based on the five principles of the Meiji emperor of Japan, which are:

1. Do not anger
2. Do not worry
3. Be grateful
4. Work hard
5. Be kind to others

Dr. Usui recommended the promotion of peace and harmony, and taught that the above precepts are keys for a healthy life. He taught his system of Reiki to more than 2000 people in his lifetime and died after suffering a stroke on March 9, 1926, four years after he began his teachings. Over the last century, Reiki has been adapted into various cultural traditions around the world.

Theory

Reiki practitioners believe that something called "life force energy" gives life to beings on Earth. Low life force energy means more stress and sickness. High life force energy means health and happiness. Reiki practitioners claim that this modality is effective for healing every known illness and affliction and that the effects of a Reiki session are always beneficial.

Reiki is not traditionally taught in a school. Rather, the ability is transferred to the student through attunement given by a Reiki master. Being attuned offers the student the ability to tap into unlimited life force energy, improving their health and quality of life. The Reiki attunement involves the Reiki Master channeling energies into the student. This process is believed to be guided by the Rei, or "God-consciousness," which is claimed to make the appropriate energetic adjustments in the process, depending on the needs of each student.

Distant Reiki attunement involves giving the practitioner the ability to use Reiki over a vast distance. This type of Reiki is claimed to not provide the complete benefit or initiation since important frequencies are left out of distant attunements.

Intellectual capacity and spiritual development are not essential to use Reiki. It is commonly considered to be a spiritual practice in nature, although it is not considered to be a religion because there is nothing that must be believed to understand Reiki. Rather, the theory is that Reiki puts people more in touch with the experience of their religion, beyond the intellectual conception thereof. In Reiki, healing the spirit by consciously deciding to improve oneself is a necessary part of the healing experience. And for healing to have a lasting effect, the patient must accept responsibility for his or her healing by taking part in it.

Practice

The practice of Reiki is simple, natural and safe for spiritual healing and self-improvement. Anyone can be subject to this practice. Patients treated by Reiki claim to feel a wonderful glowing radiance flow through them and around them during treatment. The treatment is meant to transform the whole of the being, affecting body, emotions, mind and spirit. The objectively beneficial effects of Reiki include relaxation, feelings of peace, security and wellbeing. Some claim to have received miraculous results from Reiki sessions, although it is difficult to translate such perceptions into modern, scientific terms.

The experience of Reiki is subjective, changeable and sometimes subtle. Patients often experience heat emanating from the practitioner's hands, or subtle waves or pulsations throughout the body. A typical comment from patients is how comforting they find the experience to be, and sometimes patients fall into a deep, sleep-like, meditative state. Reiki is said to be cumulative in effect, with patients achieving progressively deeper experiences. Many claim to notice changes continue to unfold even after their Reiki sessions.

Traditional Therapies

The Reiki palm healing technique transfers "universal energy" through the palms of the practitioner and into the patient, to encourage emotional or physical healing. Moments of touch from a Reiki-trained practitioner are said to bring comfort in an acute or emergency situation. There is no typical setting for Reiki, although a quiet place is preferable. The session is conducted with a fully-clothed recipient who is lying on a treatment table or sitting, supported comfortably in a chair. Light, non-invasive touch is used, with the practitioner's hands placed and held over a series of locations on the head and torso (both front and back). The placement of the hands should never be intrusive or inappropriate, nor should there be any pressure in the touch. The practitioner can also hold their hands directly above the body if needed or preferred. Additional placements on the limbs can be done as necessitated by the ailments of the individual patient.

In Modern Medicine

Reiki is said by practitioners to work in conjunction with all other medical and therapeutic techniques to relieve side effects and promote recovery. Some physicians agree that it helps promote wellbeing; however, clinical research has not overwhelmingly shown Reiki to be effective as a health care treatment for any particular type of condition.

Modern health care considers it a pseudoscience because there is no empirical evidence that the life force described in Reiki exists. Research into Reiki has been poorly designed and prone to bias. Results vary in reliability or validity, and the same healer can produce different outcomes in different studies.

Conversely, one study, Lee, Pittler and Ernst 2008 review, showed that no study in the review reported any adverse effects. According to the American Medical Association, it is inadvisable to substitute proven treatments for life-threatening conditions with unproven, alternative modalities like

Reiki, since there is no regulation of the practitioners of Reiki and no central authority controlling the use of the words *Reiki* or *Reiki Master*.

"A disciplined mind leads to happiness, and an undisciplined mind leads to suffering." — Dalai Lama

Traditional Western Alternative Modalities

The four alternate systems to contemporary medicinal practice are naturopathy, homeopathy, osteopathy and chiropractic. A review of the historical backgrounds and current status of these systems leads to the conclusion that they differ in a variety of areas, including treatment modalities, historical backgrounds, occupational development and their approach to health care.

Homeopathy, osteopathy and chiropractic emerged as distinct approaches to healing late in the nineteenth century. However, a common paradigm of treatment underlies these four alternate approaches to healing: they all generally eschew the use of synthetic pharmaceuticals and invasive treatments and they accept an indigenous theory of disease and a belief in the healing power of nature. They believe that healing and health must be self-engendered, meaning that responsibility for health rests on the patient and his or her actions, not completely within the hands, skills or power of the healer.

Chiropractic

"Rooted in Mystical Concepts"

History

D.D. Palmer founded the first chiropractic practice in the 1890s. He claims to have received his knowledge of this practice from "the other world," and his son, B.J. Palmer helped him to expand this practice. Palmer Sr. referred to it a "science of healing without drugs."[13] Its origins lie in a folk modality called "bone setting." The term "chiropractic" stems from the Greek words *cheir* (meaning hand) and *praxis* (meaning practice). It is a treatment performed centrally by hand.

Theory

Palmer hypothesized that vertebral joint misalignments, which he termed *vertebral subluxations*, interfered with the body's normal function and ability to heal itself by causing altered nerve vibration—either too tense or too slack, affecting the tone (health) of the end organ. Palmer theorized that the nervous system controlled health and therefore subluxation is the sole cause of disease. His conclusion was that manipulation is the cure

---

[13] http://enacademic.com/dic.nsf/enwiki/11532667

for all diseases of the human race. He claimed that knowledge of innate intelligence was not essential to the competent practice of chiropractic.

Generally categorized as a complementary and alternative medicine (CAM), chiropractic spinal manipulation appears to mainly benefit patients with lower-back pain, headaches, neck pain, joint conditions and disorders stemming from whiplash. Chiropractic focuses is on the relationship between the structure of the body, via the spine and adjoining features, and how the body functions, via the nervous system.

Practice

The primary focus of chiropractic is on performing adjustments (manipulations) to the spine, joints and soft tissues of the body. This is known in chiropractic as spinal manipulation therapy (SMT).

The primary goals of chiropractic adjustment are:

- Correcting alignment
- Alleviating pain
- Improving function
- Supporting the body's natural healing ability

The first visit with a chiropractor will typically include a physical examination with special emphasis on the spine. X-rays and others tests may be performed and a treatment plan will be developed from the results of these examinations. During the follow-up visits, practitioners will perform one or more of the many different types of manual therapies typical of chiropractic care. The practitioner will use their hands or a device to apply a controlled, rapid force to a joint, with the goal of increasing range and quality of motion in the area being treated.

There are two main factions in chiropractic therapy known as "straights" and "mixers." Straights emphasize vitalism, innate intelligence and spinal adjustments. They consider vertebral subluxations to be the primary cause of disease. These practitioners are now in the minority of this modality. They prefer to remain distinct from allopathic medicine.

Mixers are more open to allopathic medical techniques, and use more variations in their practice, such as exercise, stretching, massage and ice therapy, electrical muscle stimulation, therapeutic ultrasound, and moist heat. Some mixers also use other alternative medicine techniques such as nutritional supplements, acupuncture, homeopathy, herbal remedies and biofeedback. Common side effects of chiropractic can include temporary headaches, tiredness and soreness.

In Modern Medicine

Chiropractic has historically been perceived as a controversial practice, mainly due to its public stance against vaccination as an effective public health intervention. Nevertheless, it has recently gained more acceptance among conventional physicians and health plans around the world because of the more modern inclination towards the "mixer" branch of chiropractic.

The National Health Interview Survey in the US estimates that about 11% of the population receive chiropractic or osteopathic manipulation every year. In an analysis on the use of complementary health approaches for back pain, the NHIS found that chiropractic was the most commonly used therapy by far.[14] Many chiropractors describe themselves as primary care providers, although their clinical training does not support the requirements to be considered as such.

The foundation of chiropractic treatments is at odds with mainstream medicine, which has not found evidence that chiropractic manipulation is effective, other than possibly for sub-acute or chronic back pain relief. It has proven ineffective for acute back pain. There is not sufficient data to show that chiropractic manipulations are safe, and it is frequently associated with mild to moderate adverse effects, as well as serious or fatal complications in rare instances. The main danger is in the risk of vertebral artery dissection from cervical manipulation.

---

[14] Ndetan H, Evans MW, Hawk C, Walker C. Chiropractic or osteopathic manipulation for children in the United States: an analysis of data from the 2007 National Health Interview Survey. J Altern Complement Med 2012;18:347-53.

Spinal manipulation has been studied by researchers for a number of conditions like asthma, carpal tunnel syndrome and fibromyalgia, but the main focus has been on low-back pain. Modern medicine states that there is no evidence to support the claims that musculoskeletal disorders affect general health via the nervous system.

Naturopathy

"Life Knowledge from the Gods"

History

Naturopathic principles were first used in the Hippocratic School of Medicine in about 400 BC.

The Greek philosopher Hippocrates believed in viewing the person as a whole in regards to finding the causes of disease, and in using the laws of nature to induce a cure. It was from this original school of thought that Naturopathy takes its principles.

The term "naturopath" comes from the Latin *natura* (meaning birth) and *pathos* (meaning suffering). Together, the term is meant to suggest "natural healing." It is a practice based in vitalism and folk medicine, rather than what is known as "evidence-based health care."

As a formal health care practice, naturopathy has its roots in the 19th-century 'Age of Homeopathy' and the natural cure movement happening in Europe. The term "naturopathy" was coined in 1895 by John Scheel, then purchased by Benedict Lust, who is considered to be the "father of U.S. naturopathy." Lust had received schooling in hydrotherapy and went to the US to spread his drugless methods. He described naturopathy as a broad discipline, including techniques like hydrotherapy, herbal medicine, homeopathy, and eliminating toxins from the diet. Lust's views were also spiritual and he described the body as absolutely reliant on the cosmic forces of man's nature. Lust founded the American School of Naturopathy in 1901 and subsequently opened a series of schools in the first three decades of the 20th century. Several of these schools offered both Doctor of Naturopathy and Doctor of Chiropractic degrees

The advent of penicillin and other new medicines resulted in the sharp rise in the popularity of modern medicine and contributed to the temporary decline of naturopathy. Throughout the 20th century, health care associations around the world campaigned against naturopathy and other heterodox medical systems (at variance with the official or orthodox health care positions of the time), recommending the revocation of licenses to practice naturopathic medicine, largely succeeding for a time. Then, in the 1970s, a revival of interest occurred with the holistic health movement in the U.S. and Canada because patients found appeal in the nature-based aspects of the modality.[15]

Theory

Naturopathic medicine primarily serves to promote self-healing. Proponents believe that modern technology, environmental pollution, poor diet, and stress each play significant roles in the degradation of health. Naturopathic physicians generally complete a 4-year, graduate-level program at an accredited medical school. They must pass an exit exam to receive their license and fulfill annual continuing education requirements. Some allopathic physicians and health care providers have pursued additional training in naturopathic treatments to take a more integrative approach to patient health. Traditional naturopaths receive non-accredited educations from a variety of sources and are not eligible for licensing at present time.

Practice

The principles of naturopathy are founded on the belief in:

1. The healing power of nature — recognizing the inherent self-healing process that is ordered and intelligent. This includes identifying and removing obstacles to healing and recovery.

---

[15] Gale, Nicola. *The Sociology of Traditional, Complementary and Alternative Medicine.* Wiley-Blackwell Open Online, 2014

2. Identifying and treating the causes — removing the underlying causes of illness rather than focusing on symptoms. These can be physical or mental.
3. Doing no harm — not using treatments that may create other conditions. This includes:
   1. Using medical substances that have minimal risk of harmful side effects, and methods that use the least for necessary to diagnose and treat
   2. Avoiding the harmful suppression of symptoms
   3. Working with the individual's self-healing process
4. Seeing the naturopath as the teacher — educating patients about taking their health in their hands through teaching self-care
5. Treating the whole person — taking into account the individual's physical, mental, emotional, genetic, environmental, social, and spiritual states
6. Preventing disease — assessing risk factors, heredity and susceptibility to disease and removing toxic substances and situations from a patient's lifestyle to prevent the further onset of disease

Traditional Therapies

A naturopath is often the last resort in the search for health. They typically practice in a freelance environment, working in hospitals, spas, or research clinics. Today, there are a growing number of health care clinics that employ naturopaths alongside nutritionists and other modalities in a joint-healing effort of patients.

A consultation with a naturopath typically involves a detailed interview on lifestyle, medical history, emotional tone, and physical features. They mainly focus on a holistic approach, often completely foregoing the use of surgery or drugs. Naturopaths often position themselves to be primary care providers and at times prescribe drugs and perform minor surgery. Traditional naturopaths deal exclusively with advocating for lifestyle changes, without diagnosing or treating disease. They do not generally recommend vaccines and antibiotics but they may provide alternative remedies to these illnesses.

Typical methods practiced by naturopaths include: herbalism, homeopathy, acupuncture, physical medicine, applied kinesiology, colonic enemas, chelation therapy, psychotherapy, hygiene, reflexology, acupuncture, bio-resonance, ozone therapy, massage therapy, and Traditional Chinese Medicine. They may also prescribe natural cures like sunshine, fresh air, heat or cold, and nutritional advice like fasting, whole food or a vegetarian diet. Physical medicine like manipulative therapy, exercise and sports medicine are also prescribed, as well as psychological counseling, including meditation and relaxation for stress management.

In Modern Medicine

Naturopathy is known as an alternative or pseudoscientific medicine by the allopathic medical community and is considered to be ineffective and possibly harmful. Practitioners of naturopathic medicine have been found criminally liable in courts of law around the world. According to the American Cancer Society, "scientific evidence does not support claims that naturopathic medicine can cure cancer or any other disease."[16] Nevertheless, naturopathic doctors choose to label themselves medical professionals. As of 2009, 15 U.S. states plus Puerto Rico, the US Virgin Islands and the District of Columbia all began licensing naturopathic doctors. The practice of naturopathy is still prohibited in some states.[17]

Doctor Of Osteopathic Medicine

"Doctors that DO"

History

Osteopathic medicine was established in Kirksville, Missouri, in the late 1800s by medical doctor Andrew Taylor Still who saw his contemporaries doing more harm than good to their patients. Frequent use of caustic and/or toxic medicinal substances and dangerous surgeries were typical

---

[16] Srivastava, Amit Kishor. Pharmacology: A Book Of Achieving Knowledge For Drugs. Educreation Publishing, 2011.
[17] https://aanmc.org/resources/licensure/

of medicine at the time. His focus became to develop a system of medical care that would promote what he saw to be the body's innate ability to heal itself. Osteopathic medicine is considered by some to be a social movement and it is often referred to as the "jazz of medicine," a term coined by Dr. Wolfgang Gilliar, DO (osteopathic physicians are known as DOs.)[18]

Theory

Osteopathy is a form of diagnosis and treatment that focuses mainly on the muscles and joints of the body. The focus of osteopathic medicine is to help each person achieve a high level of wellness by focusing on health promotion and disease prevention. DOs work to break down the barriers to good health that we erect in our everyday actions by working in partnership with patients to understand their individual lives.

The osteopathic philosophy is to look at the whole person, rather than a simple collection of organ systems and body parts that may become injured or diseased. This holistic approach to patient care turns the patient into a partner in their own health care process. As a result, DOs are trained to communicate with people from diverse backgrounds on a number of issues that go beyond the traditional purview of allopathic medicine. DOs believe that there is more to good health than the absence of pain or disease. They consider themselves to be 'guardians of wellness'. They seek to gain a deeper understanding of their patient's lifestyle and environment, rather than only treating symptoms. They are trained to listen and to get to know their patient as a whole person.

Practice

Osteopathic medicine is a branch of modern medicine that provides all of the same benefits as allopathic medicine, such as prescription drugs, surgery, and the use of technology to diagnose disease and evaluate injury. The added benefits of osteopathic medicine are the hands-on diagnoses and a system of treatment known as osteopathic manipulative therapy (OMT), which involves using the hands to diagnose, treat, and prevent

---

[18] https://www.revolvy.com/page/Osteopathic-medicine

illness or injury. Using OMT, an osteopathic physician will move muscles and joints using techniques that include stretching, gentle pressure and resistance. This is an empathetic approach to medicine that is practiced according to the latest scientific information, sometimes using cutting-edge technology. They also consider options to complement pharmaceuticals and surgery. DOs conduct clinical and basic scientific research to help advance the frontiers of medicine and to demonstrate the effectiveness of the osteopathic approach to patient care.

Today, the training of osteopathic physicians is distinct from that of their MD counterparts due to emphasis placed on viewing the patient as a whole person, with four key principles central to the care of all patients:

1. The body is a unit of mind, body and spirit.
2. The body is capable of self-regulation, self healing, and health maintenance.
3. Structure and Function are reciprocally interrelated.
4. Rational treatment is based upon these basic principles.

All conventional methods of allopathic diagnosis and treatment are used, with additional emphasis placed on a return to normal body mechanics as central to maintaining good health.

Traditional Therapies

Hands-on techniques help alleviate pain, restore motion, support the body's natural functions and influence the body's structure. The idea behind this treatment is the use of "healing touch." Osteopathic medicine purports that OMT can also help patients with a number of health problems that include:

- asthma
- sinus disorders
- carpal tunnel syndrome
- migraines
- menstrual pain

OMT can complement and sometimes even replace drugs or surgery. In this way, OMT brings an important dimension to standard medical care.

In Modern Medicine

DOs are licensed to practice the full scope of medicine in all 50 states. It is a branch of the medical profession practiced primarily in the United States, and is a recognized branch of medicine in 65 other countries.

The main goal for osteopathic medical schools is to produce primary care physicians, believing that a strong foundation in primary care makes one a better physician, regardless of the speciality they may eventually practice. More than 1/3 of osteopathic medical graduates choose a career in primary care, most of which practice in rural and urban underserved areas. Nearly 1 in 5 medical students in the US are attending an osteopathic medical school and more than 5,400 new osteopathic physicians enter the workforce each year.

The Doctor of Osteopathic Medicine (D.O.) degree is equivalent to the Doctor of Medicine (MD) degree and there are more than 100,000 DOs in the US in every medical specialty.

Brain-Centered Healing Modalities

"Satisfaction of one's curiosity is one of the greatest sources of happiness in life." — Linus Pauling

We have learned from the long-established scientific practices of psychology and psychiatry that they are disciplines that have been in constant flux throughout history. Many factions have broken away from the main streams of psychiatry and psychology at every turn to champion their slight deviation based on new understandings. Rather than go into the whole of either field in depth, we will briefly explain what all three schools of understanding the psyche have to say in regards to affecting the whole of the body's system.

Psychology

Psychology is the science of behavior as connected to the mind. It is a study of conscious and unconscious phenomena, including feeling and thought. An academic discipline of immense scope, psychologists seek to understand the phenomena manifested by the brain. It is a social science that aims to understand individuals and groups by establishing general principles through researching specific cases.

The majority of psychologists are involved in a therapeutic role as counselor or clinician.

Psychological knowledge is applied to the assessment and treatment of mental health problems, as well as understanding and solving problems in society. Many psychologists are involved in scientific research related to mental processes and behavior, typically working in a university or hospital setting. Other settings include industrial and organizational, human development and aging, sports, health, media, forensic and law.

Psychologists study if and how mental functions might be localized in the brain and the biopsychological model is an integrated perspective toward understanding consciousness, behavior, and social interaction. This model assumes that any given behavior or mental process affects and is affected by biological, psychological, and social factors—all of which are said to be dynamically interrelated.

Behaviorism

Human behavior is a major area of study in psychology. Behavioral research is conducted in order to improve techniques for behavior modification. Behavioral Psychologists use stimuli on their subjects (some might call them patients) to create associations with pain or pleasure in order to change behavior over time.

"There can be no moral warrant for studying man's nature unless the study will enable us to control his acts." — Thorndike (1911)

Cognitive Theory

Cognitive psychology and psychoanalysis studies the mental processes that underlie mental activity such as perception, attention reasoning, thinking, problem solving, memory, learning, language and emotion. This branch uses new technologies like computer simulations to perform experimental research on test subjects, linking psychological phenomena with the structure and function of the brain. Psychologists have classified a thorough catalogue of cognitive biases out of this research.

Humanistic Theory

Humanistic psychology from the 1950s sought to glimpse the whole person, focusing on uniquely human issues such as free will, personal growth, self-actualization, self-identity, death, aloneness, freedom, and meaning. It respects the worth of persons and their differences of approaches in the exploration of new aspects of human behavior. It is the "third force" in contemporary psychology, concerned with more abstract theories and systems like love, creativity, self, growth, organism, basic need-gratification, self-actualization, higher values, being, becoming, spontaneity, play, humor, affection, naturalness, warmth, ego-transcendence, objectivity, autonomy, responsibility, meaning, fair-play, transcendental experience, peak experience, courage, and other related concepts.

Over time, the discipline of psychology has evolved to accept each of the three major divisions of psychology as a part of the whole. Dr.

Martin Seligman, founding editor-in-chief of the American Psychological Association electronic journal *Prevention and Treatment*, said that if you push a dog too far with behavior modification, they will develop something called "learned helplessness" that doesn't fall under the scope of behaviorism[19], even if you can teach a dog new tricks by using treats and cues. Psychologists in the field of public health use a wide variety of interventions to influence human behavior. These range from public relations campaigns and outreach, to governmental laws and policies. Psychologists study the composite influence of all these different tools in an effort to influence whole populations of people.

Psychiatry

Psychiatry is a field of medicine that is primarily focused on the mind but includes the body and overall well-being into an integrative picture. Its goal is to study, prevent, and treat mental disorders in humans. Psychiatrists try to mediate between the perspectives of general society and that of the mentally ill to find the balance that can reconnect their patient with the rest of society. Psychiatry lies somewhere between neurology and psychology, differing from other mental health modalities in that practitioners are required to understand both the social and biological sciences. Psychiatry practitioners study the body's systems and organs, the patient's individual life experiences and the physical health of the patient for a holistic, integrative view of the patient.

The mental disorders that psychiatry treats can be divided into three general categories:

1. mental illnesses
2. severe learning disabilities
3. personality disorders

Although its focus has stayed the same over time, the diagnostic and treatment processes of psychiatry continue to evolve. The field of psychiatry

[19] http://www.associationofanimalbehaviorprofessionals.com/vol3no1.pdf

has become more biological, linking it more closely to other medical sciences.

Psychiatrists often work with other disciplines in the research and treatment processes. Treatment typically includes a combination of medication and therapy, supplemented by a wide variety of modalities that can include supported employment, community reinforcement, and assertive community treatment. Psychiatrists will consult with mental health counselors, social workers, public health specialists, etc., to diagnose and treat their patients with an integrative approach.

Psychoanalysis

Sigmund Freud is thought to be the father of the psychological theories and therapeutic techniques that are defined as psychoanalysis. The central belief of psychoanalysis is that all people have unconscious thoughts, feelings, desires, and memories. To understand a patient's present state of mind, the unconscious mind must be brought into conscious awareness. Only then is a patient able to find catharsis from psychological disturbances and distress. Our unconscious motivations influence behavior and our personalities are highly influenced by events in early childhood, usually set by the ages of five to seven. The conflicts between the conscious and the unconscious mind often lead to emotional and psychological problems like depression and anxiety. Dream analysis and free association techniques are used to diagnose problems in the unconscious mind.

Freud's theory of the human mind being composed of the id, the ego, and the superego changed how we think about the human mind and behavior. Erik Erikson was another theorist associated with the evolution of psychoanalysis by stressing the importance of growth throughout a person's lifespan. Today, psychoanalysis have evolved to include applied psychoanalysis, which applies psychoanalytic principles to real-world settings and situations. Psychoanalysts also use neuroscience to psychoanalyze topics such as dreams and repression. Modern approaches to psychoanalytic therapy have moved away from Freudian rhetoric to a nonjudgmental and empathetic approach. Research has also demonstrated that the self-examination utilized in the psychoanalytic process can help contribute to long-term emotional growth.

Despite its critics, psychoanalysis played an important role in the development of psychology. It influenced our approach to the treatment of mental health issues and continues to exert an influence in psychology to this day. Psychoanalysis opened up a new view on mental illness, suggesting that talking about problems with a professional could help relieve symptoms of psychological distress.

Cutting Edge Medical Theories

Forward-thinking companies in today's world of health technology are implementing old health care technology in new formats. At the 2018 Wired Health Conference, presenters suggested that the more scientific communities begin to understand interconnectivity in the body, the less focus there will be on researching new technology in clinical settings. Clinics can be free to focus more attention on innovating efficient uses of current technology and capitalizing on recent big inventions. Many new technologies are not miracle cures, but they are providing a new edge to the health industry. Theories that have long been uncovered are finally being understood. Brain stimulating technology, for instance, was first uncovered by NASA in 1972—but they didn't realize it at the time. Researchers are only now being able to apply these theories after decades of gaining the necessary understanding about the body's individual systems and what they do.

Data Revolution

Pamela Spence, Global Life Sciences Industry Leader, suggests that the health world is currently immersed in the fourth industrial revolution along with the rest of the world. She suggests that the key to unlocking this "revolution" is data. Prior to the Internet Age, clinicians used to be supported by data scientists. Increasingly, though, data scientists are being supported by clinicians. Data is easier than ever to capture, and processing power is growing exponentially every year. But health care data is currently spread out among many different providers of health services. The dream of the future of medicine in the health-tech industry is to collate data from across different platforms and harness that information for the collective good of all.

New health-tech companies are also working to serve the greater good by giving their users full ownership of their data, as mined by the company as part of their service. One such company is Heterogenous, who provide a gene sequencing service where the user is able to select which research projects their data can be made available to anonymously. Most companies of the old ways sell their user data to third parties without informing the customer (a completely legal process) while new health tech companies appear to want to be open and collaborative.

Individualized Medicine

One of the newest disciplines in modern health care is known as Personalized Medicine. Bruce Levine's CAR-T cell therapy retrains a patient's own cells to target a health issue, like in the case of cancer cells. These types of personalized interventions are tailored to the individual in the way that an organ transplant is carefully selected for the precise patient—by looking at the patients genetics. Scientists have recently discovered that just like with our genes or our blood, our voices possess "biomarkers," or patterns indicative of abnormality or disease. Using this technology, we are able to detect, with a high degree of accuracy, illnesses like depression, diabetes and cardiovascular disease.

Wearable Technologies

New approaches to old problems are involving new understandings about the human psyche. In the case of obesity, for example, due to thousands of years of facing starvation, our bodies evolved to make it very difficult for us to lose weight. New devices, like the Modius, stimulate brain nerves to encourage the body to move towards a more optimal state. In the case of the Modius, this involves stimulating the eighth cranial nerve in the hypothalamus, which reduces appetite and increases the body's potential for weight loss. 30 years ago, there was not much that could be done about severe heart disease. But as new technologies like stents and heart surgery developed, new interventions can be made for patients.

The traditional model of test administrators working long hours in a lab over long periods of time is over. Studies can now be carried out over vast distances and with millions of patients in their own homes using wearable sensors. This type of data is more accurate (conducted in the comfort of the home, rather than a lab) and performed at rates that were previously unimaginable within a clinical setting. Wearable sensors are already being used in a number of clinical settings, such as in sleep assessment.

Remote Treatments

Time is of the essence when it comes to diagnosing an issue. Innovative companies are working on alternatives to traditional treatments that save on time, effort/pain, and money. 3-D printing technology solves the problem of frequent doctor visits to refit a plaster cast by providing a lightweight, waterproof, tailored alternative that can be printed in seconds. Liquid biopsies are another alternative that can see cancer screening becoming a routine check during an annual checkup, rather than waiting for an appointment with a specialist.

Wireless Solutions

App-based solutions are another new big part of the tech world. Applications downloaded to our smart devices can make health care accessible to millions of people worldwide. Apps are quick to rise to ubiquity and they are a potentially powerful tools for the good of humanity's health. Clinova's app Caidr helps users to "distinguish minor ailments from a more serious illness," according to their website description. Designed by two pharmacists, the app asks a series of simple questions in order to assess if the user should visit a doctor, or whether a pharmacist could offer effective over-the-counter medications. An app such as this could take pressure off wait times to see a doctor and save patient money. Other apps, like Kry, allow for users to speak directly with a doctor. It is already a part of Sweden's health service, where 2% of all primary care appointments take place through the app.

With the help of technology, doctors are making house calls again, yet they are not needing to leave their offices. Through telemedicine—the treating of patients via satellite, video conferencing, data transfer, etc—medical records are increasingly inclusive of video and audio files for contextual media. Patients now have greater flexibility for seeking treatment, not needing to book time to travel for an appointment. Doctors can also treat more patients, with more frequency, especially in cases of chronic disease management or post-ICU care. Sharing information between medical specialists in a multidisciplinary, "integrative" health care approach becomes much easier and more timely through the use of technology.

Having an 'Internet of Things' for health care means that patients and doctors can potentially:

- Remotely configure medical devices, including predictive maintenance
- Remote monitor patient vitals
- Host pre-surgical virtual and augmented assessments

The Cutting Edge In Alternative And Allopathic Medicine

Two new branches of medicine, Functional Medicine and Bioelectronic Medicine, take advantage of many of the forward-thinking solutions in the above health-tech list of advancements. They are harnessing new technologies and using them alongside old understanding to create personalized solutions for patients, built on a comprehensive understanding of each patient's individual data set. Functional Medicine is considered to be a more alternative theory for its focus on root causes; Bioelectronic Medicine is a more allopathic branch of modern medicine, full of promise but still under the radar for many health care seekers and practitioners. Again, this is not meant to be an exhaustive list of the modern health care modalities available, but a small, select representation intended to pique your interest to search more on your own.

Functional Medicine

Functional Medicine is a branch of modern, alternative medicine that works to determine how and why illness occurs. It seeks to restore health by addressing the root causes of disease for each individual. To do this, FM practitioners require a detailed understanding of each patient's genetic, biochemical, and lifestyle factors, using this data to create a personalized treatment plan. Practitioners focus on the interactions between a patient's environment and their gastrointestinal, endocrine, and immune systems.

Practitioners of FM claim that it leads to improved patient outcomes. According to the Institute of Functional Medicine's website, the treatment of chronic diseases accounted for 86% of all health care costs in 2015. FM claims to have better outcomes than allopathic medicine and lower health care costs. The IFM claim to bring dramatic results to patients who have previously received unsuccessful treatments.

The practice of FM involves using a variety of diagnostics, therapeutics, and prevention strategies. Practitioners design nutritional and lifestyle interventions aimed to improve patient compliance and outcomes, and they use innovative assessment tools to diagnose and treat illness from an FM approach. The goal is to establish a mutually empowering partnership between clinician and patient to obtain the most honest and open answers from the patient. By combining scientific rigor with patient-centered pragmatism, FM has resolved illnesses that were conventionally thought to be untreatable.

Each diagnosis in FM may be one of many contributing to an individual's illness, and each symptom may be an indicator of many diseases/diagnoses. The precise manifestation of each cause depends on the individual's genes, environment, and lifestyle. According to FM, treatments that address the right cause are the only treatments that will having lasting benefit beyond symptom suppression.

FM addresses seven core imbalances. They are: hormonal and neurotransmitter, oxidation reduction, detoxification, immune and inflammatory, digestive, structural, and mind-body/body-mind imbalances. Jeffrey Bland, founder of the Institute of Functional Medicine, says the five principles of healing these core imbalances are:

1. Correct the precipitating factor and control oxidative stress.
2. Get rid of sources of chronic inflammation.
3. Manage the folate cycle.
4. Regulate hormones.
5. Manage insulin and control blood sugar.

To find these core imbalances, three tools in the symptom mapping process: the Functional medicine Matrix, the Timeline, and the GoToIt framework.

FM Matrix — Using a patient's thorough personal, family, social, and medical history to organize each patient's health issues into priorities, the FM Matrix categorizes seemingly disparate issues into a complete story of the complex individual causes of disease in a patient.

FM Timeline — A patient's history that gives insight into the effects of previous life events, with the goal of motivating the patient to change by participating in the treatment is the FM Timeline. It is a graphic representation of factors that predispose, provoke, and contribute to pathological changes and dysfunctional results in a patient. This helps practitioners to see the relationships between events through the patient's whole lifespan—from preconception to the present.

GOTOIT — Standing for Gather, Organize, Tell, Order, Initiate, and Track, GOTOIT helps practitioners establish rapport with their patients; to identify unhealthy patterns and to propose personalized lifestyle modifications.

FM evolved from a small group of influential thought leaders who realized the importance of an individualized approach to the causes of disease based on evolving research in nutritional science, genomics, and epigenetics. Clinicians use low-risk interventions to modify molecular and cellular systems, to reverse the root causes of disease. They look for unifying factors at the cellular and systems levels that underlie organism-wide problems. The approach became systematized so that it can be taught to a wider group of practitioners from differing backgrounds, sharing maps that link symptoms to the root processes that cause illness.

FM Practitioners suggest that conventional allopathic medicine is dysfunctional because it does not deal with underlying causes of symptoms. Nevertheless, critics of Functional Medicine suggest that this theory includes a number of unproven and disproven techniques. According to oncologist Dr. David Gorski, the vagueness of FM is a deliberate tactic to make it easier to promote the discipline. He claims that it centers around unnecessary and expensive testing procedures. FM also espouses principles that are considered to be myths by allopathic medicine, such as diet and lifestyle will prevent and treat most disease, or the concept of ultra-wellness (that we should aim for better than normal). FM Practitioners also treat "non-diseases" like yeast, adrenal fatigue, toxicity requiring detoxification, and leaky gut.

Dr. Peter Osborne is known as the first allopathic doctor to identify diet, specifically grains, as a leading cause of chronic suffering. Known as the "Gluten-free Warrior," Dr. Osborne practices functional medicine, finding the origins of a disease instead of simply treating the symptoms. In his experience, the origin is often gluten (especially the hidden sources of gluten) in our diets. Dr. Osborne uses a combination of gluten-free diet and supplementation and has eliminated chronic pain in thousands of his patients.

Bioelectronic Medicine

Bioelectronic Medicine is a new allopathic approach to diagnosing and treating disease and injury. The science behind Bioelectronic Medicine suggests that because the body's major organs are innervated, the brain is able to monitor and regulate organ function. BM makes use of a team of experts from neurophysiology, neuroscience, molecular and cell biology, and bioengineering. Device technology is used to read and modulate electrical energy in the body's nervous system, which opens the doors to real-time diagnosis and treatment through either nerve-blocking or nerve-stimulation devices. Devices are already being used in clinical trials to treat inflammatory diseases such as rheumatoid arthritis.

The purpose of BM is to identify physiological triggers and develop new research tools in order to develop a medical device technology that uses neural pathways for the treatment of a specific disease or injury. Practitioners of BM are currently working hard to understand the language of the nervous system in order to perform advanced diagnostics.

The United States' DARPA program recently launched a program called ElectRx to fund research on electrical treatments for various diseases. It aims to make it easier to deliver electrical stimulation in a minimally invasive and precisely targeted way. In the long run, BM can be more effective and less expensive to develop than pharmaceuticals. According to its proponents, BM device technology is also easier to administer, non-toxic, more precise, 100% compliant, and involves minimal health risks and side effects.

The Feinstein Institute for Medical Research is a part of research enterprise Northwell Health — a collaborative effort in advancing science to prevent disease and cure patients. 1,500+ scientists and researchers have made important discoveries in many medical fields. Their motto is "successful inventions require more than just the idea; they require solidarity, tenacity, dedication and time." Feinstein is a unique organization that breeds a sense of responsibility to innovate and grow, keeping an eye on future cures in an environment of collaboration. Kevin J. Tracey, MD, President and CEO of Feinstein, says that collaboration is "essential to improving the health and happiness of future societies."

BM is still not a widely used technology, with current therapeutic devices still so large that they stimulate an entire nerve, rather than targeting a small fraction of nerve fibers. However, the implications are significant for medical acupuncture, and researchers have demonstrated effect in treating migraines and carpal tunnel syndrome.

Dr. Walter J. Urban with Alexandra Luty

Biological Medicine

Patients who turn to the modern modality Biological Medicine are generally coming after years of treatment with drugs, surgery or radiation, too often with little real benefit. In fact, their conventional treatment has commonly caused them great suffering. The view of this modality is that the natural state of the body is 'health'. Outside factors, like toxins, stress and poor nutrition, impair the body's regulatory systems. Biological Medicine recognizes that the body has a lifelong power to heal and regenerate by focusing on the unique story of each patient and learning the original cause of the disorder.

Healing is done using natural methods that includes assessing the body's entire combination of physical, mental, emotional, and spiritual factors and identifying which combination of these factors may be causing the body to be out of balance. Practitioners use the self-healing powers of the body to initiate healing and promote restoration of balance.

The fundamental concepts of maintaining health in Biological Medicine are:

1. Regulating blockages
2. Preventing toxic overload
3. Recognizing that disease has multiple causes
4. A person's constitution has influence over health
5. Disruptive focuses in the body have influence over health
6. The reactive capability of cells have influence over health
7. Nutrition is the principal factor in treatment
8. The intestines and intestinal flora have influence over health

Detoxification, intestinal and immune system health, and regeneration are the three pillars of health care in Biological Medicine. The goals is to reverse degenerative activity and promote long-term healing. Treatments are generally non-invasive and they rarely require the use of prescription drugs.

Conclusions About Modalities Of Health Care

For those who take the time to do further study, you will be able to better understand the benefits, limitations and dangers of each of these modalities. This information is important to know for both patients and healers. We are all subject to disease and old age, and the more we know, the better we can conduct our lives.

An extreme example of a personal lack of information about a new modality was when I received a diagnostic procedure called a tilt test for my heart. Before the test was administered, I was required to sign a document acknowledging that I may die from taking the test. It was explained to me that this was a routine procedure and that I had nothing to be concerned about. I hesitantly signed the document. The test administrator then asked me to lay down on a vertical board and gave me intravenous drops of nitroglycerin, after which the board was rotated for the test. When the test was complete, I got off the board and sat in the adjoining waiting room. Over the next few minutes, I started to lose my speech and then having convulsions. My tongue went in and out of my mouth uncontrollably as my body was convulsing. I was totally helpless for the next 15 to 20 minutes as my wife looked on. I was sure that my life was over. I will never take that test again and I suggest to everyone that you thoroughly investigate everything you are told to do — even by a medical professional — before you agree to be subjected to something new. Know the side effect of all drugs you are prescribed, the risks of prostate biopsies, the effects of ayurvedic herbs, extreme diets, etc.

To get the full benefit of any of the modalities we have described in this section, all of them must learn how to work together. We must not separate aspect of our health, or where we obtain information about our health. Our lives and bodies do not function in separate pieces. Each part of us is related to every other part. A holistic view of functioning rather than a reductionist view of functioning must be practiced to achieve the goal of good health and increased longevity. And we need to listen to what are bodies are telling us because they are our best guides. In my own example, an experienced massage therapist cured my scoliosis because I listened to my body's cry for massage relief.

Due to practical necessity, standard medical education takes place in a piecemeal format, where the holistic human health picture is broken down into categories of knowledge. Allopathic trainees learn about biology, for instance, separately from chemistry. Holistic training, on the other hand, is about gaining recognition of different ideas over time. We may see many medical doctors learning about nutrition and teaching it in various summit programs online, such as *The Sacred Plant* series, or the *Re-engineer Your Life Holistic Health Summit*. As our awareness increases, it becomes the responsibility of both professional and patient to learn holistic thinking and practice. Devoting time to do this must become a priority if we are to increase our lifespan and happiness.

Never forget that we are all a part of everything and our bodies function physically, mentally, emotionally and spiritually, and we are also connected to each other and the planet. When health becomes a bigger priority than money, it becomes the time to learn and actively pursue real wealth in knowledge.

NUTRITION

"The important thing is this: to be able, at any moment, to sacrifice what we are for what we could become." — Maharishi Mahesh

Do doctors give us the whole truth about our health if they don't discuss nutrition? A discussion about diet and exercise (or the lack of a healthy amount of both) between patient and practitioner is the easiest way to prevent and even recover from a vast amount of illness and health complications, and yet doctors often omit this conversation. They instead allude to it by saying things like your blood pressure or blood sugar are high because these are symptoms for which they can prescribe medicine. But as practitioners are learning more and more every day, "genetic predisposition" doesn't mean that you will succumb to that disease. Most — if not all — diseases can be prevented with diet.

The Futility Of The Fad Diets

A multitude of confusing and differing information about proper, healthy nutrition makes it difficult to make the right choices when it comes to our diets. Right now, there are 8 major fad diets proposed in the world-wide "health" industry. They include:

- Ketogenic Diet
- Raw Diet
- Vegan Diet
- Vegetarian Diet
- Paleo Diet
- 80-10-10 Diet
- High Protein (Atkin's) Diet
- John Robin's Diet for the 21st Century
- Chinese Nutrition

Evolved health care practitioners like Dr. Jack Wolfson have been giving up their lucrative allopathic practices to pursue their passions for healing. In his book, The Paleo Cardiologist (2015), Dr. Wolfson suggests eating mainly vegetables so that you microbiome — the community of microorganisms (bacteria, fungi and viruses) inside your body — is in balance within the environment of your body.

A new pathway to healing within the allopathic medicine system can be found in Dr. Pedram Shojai's groundbreaking gut health docuseries, INTERCONNECTED: The Power to Heal From Within (2018). In it, he describes how the gut's microbiome (the full collection of your gut's bacteria and system therein) is a life altering "germ shield." Hidden deep inside your gut reside hundreds of billions of germs (bacteria), which are present within all of us. They make our immune system strong, healthy, and incredibly efficient. New discoveries have gone as far as to say that if you protect the bacteria in your gut, you can boost our immunities, keep our digestive systems running smoothly, maintain balanced hormone levels, and protect overall brain function.

Finding the "right diet" for you is of great importance, but conflicting information is the norm — even from the mainstream, allopathic community. Some doctors will tell you that coffee is good for you, while others say that is is not. The same goes for eggs, meat, chocolate, raw food, and so on. Both sides—for and against — are represented by qualified authorities. So how does this affect you? Do you give up and run away from facing the conflicts? What is best for you and how do you decide?

There is no magical solution to offer. I, too, face the dilemma of 'what to eat' without any definitive answers as of this time. However, I continue to inform myself as best I can. It can be overwhelming to read and evaluate all that is available but I do so the best I can. I continue to take responsibility for my health so that I can have a clear conscience, especially when it comes to keeping away from decidedly toxic processed foods.

Dr. Ben Johnson is an allopathic doctor who is adamant about his patients taking responsibility for their own health. He recognizes that detoxification is critical and that bowel movements are great indicators of overall patient health, so he always discusses this with his patients. Our gut bacteria is critical and we need to have a good biome to digest our food and to receive nutrients. Two to three bowel movements a day are essential, according to Dr. Johnson, who says that the more time we have between movements, the more time the body has to absorb toxic chemicals from our nutrient-deficient, GMO diets. Dr. Johnson gets his patients to do colonics and liver cleanse protocols every time because he has realized over the years that we are all heavy metal toxic. We think it's normal because every day, we are touching, eating, drinking and breathing metal. He says that after years of testing his patients, he knows that everyone who is sick is heavy metal toxic so he doesn't even waste his patients' money on testing for this and goes right into treatment.

In *The Truth About Cancer* documentary series, Dr. Johnson says, "I sold my cancer clinic years ago and became involved in healing codes, which is a physical system of helping the body remove physiological stress and then the body does what it's designed to do: it heals itself. The healing codes don't heal anything. They just remove physiological stress and then the body heals itself."

We have each done the best that we can according to the beliefs about food that we were taught individually over the course of our lives. The important thing is to improve yourself by starting with a more open mind, which you are doing by reading this book. It is a difficult process to change diets for many people because change can feel threatening. It is more comfortable to stay where you have been up until now, even if you feel unhappy. Fear is a stronger motivator than happiness for many people. But with courage, taking responsibility for your health can be accomplished!

The holistic team approach can be quite useful in recognizing the early sign of a disease process; to help prevent the disease. In all of my consultations with allopathic practitioners in my life, I have never met one who advised me to eliminate sugar from my diet, or who asked me about my bowel movements. We need correct nutrition and detoxification in all areas to be able to absorb any good nutrition that our bodies receive. And we need an integrative holistic team approach to bring this information to light.

The Future Of Medicine Is Food

Why do mainstream toothpaste manufacturers put sugar in their tooth cleaning products? The number two ingredient in most toothpaste is sorbitol, which is a sugar-alcohol with a sweet taste, also known as a sugar substitute. Have you ever read the ingredients of your everyday toothpaste brand? Do you read the ingredients of what you buy to put into your mouth or on your skin? And do you study the effects of them on your body? Or do you simply trust what is on the label or packaging? Do you believe the commercials about these products?

The words "natural", "organic", and "doctor-recommended" can be very deceptive. We are conditioned to be complacent and we therefore do not feel fully responsible for our own health. This sense of complacency is not entirely your fault, since many westerners live as robotic slaves to the corporations that control these products and advertise to us in dozens of ways everyday. Most of us have been raised by generations of corporate slaves that did not know any better. Now is the time to wake up and take responsibility for your health. The time has finally come because by reading this book and others like it, you now know better. Depend on no one but yourself to find the truth, even though it may feel elusive. You cannot simply trust the doctors who advise you to know any better. Even qualified nutritionists lack knowledge about proper diet for all types. I once asked a nutritionist why the jello served to me in the hospital was green. The nutritionist didn't have an answer. I look forward to the day when sustenance given in a health care facility is purposefully full of nutrition.

Many nutritionists also advise eating protein with carbohydrates. They have never read any alternate theories of food combining. Others don't speak of the over 10,000 food additives that have disease-producing effects on our health. Even highly informed people are unable to know their best nutrition. There are so many different diets and each claims to be the correct one. New information is being offered every year. In the month of November 2018 alone, Amazon online bookstore released roughly 240 new books on the subject of diet. And that's not even an unusual month! There are literally hundreds if not thousands of books release on the topic every year!

In the 2017 book, The Plant Paradox: The Hidden Dangers in "Healthy" Foods That Cause Disease and Weight Gain, Dr. Steven Gundry, famous cardiologist and author, proposes what may be considered to be revolutionary ideas and information. In this seminal book, he turns around all previously known nutritional information. Following extensive research on the subject, Dr. Gundry discusses the effects of lectins in nutrition. Based on his research on lectins in different foods and how they are processed by the body, he lists the foods to eat and those to avoid. His books continue to be on best seller lists because of his evolutionary ideas on what he believes to be the best way to access proper nutrition.

Dr. Mark Hyman, MD, tries to resolve the conflict between paleo and vegetarian ideas in his book, Food: What The Hell Should I Eat? (2018).

He seeks to reveal which foods nurture our health and which pose a threat. According to Dr. Hyman, the role of food is to be a powerful medicine capable of reversing chronic disease. He also suggests that our food system and policies impact the environment, the economy, social justice, and personal health. Therefore, we need a holistic view of growing, cooking, and eating food in ways that nourish our bodies and the earth, while creating a healthy society at the same time.

There is a growing consensus about eliminating things like sugar, processed food, and alcohol from our diets. If reading that sentence causes you anguish, do not withdraw from your responsibility to yourself. Now is the time to learn more discipline and observe where you are in your journey towards health, rather than defending your beliefs. Open your mind to do this self-evaluation and eliminate what you need to remove from your diet to become clearer in your thinking. Do not focus your energy on defending your beliefs. Read and listen to what is available for your self development so that you can take better care of your health. Remember that no one can do this for you. Question all you read and hear but keep listening. Procrastination and avoidance are not your allies so don't use them to defend yourself. If you don't start to take more responsibility today, when will you start? It is your decision and it is your life. Increase your disease prevention and detoxification. Don't wait for the crisis because it will surely come. All of this is up to you.

Symptoms of disease take time to develop. It takes time to form a stone in one of your organs. Arteriosclerosis doesn't develop in a few days. You have made yourself sick, either knowingly or unknowingly, over time. If you know about the effects of sugar and kept eating it, you need to seek help. If you do not know about all the sugar substitutes and the hidden sugars in foods, it is time to start learning about it. The same goes for fluoride in table salt. Himalayan salt has shown to be a valuable alternative; however, when I read the ingredients on a package at the supermarket, I was shocked to find fluoride in it! Locating the causes of symptoms will take time and work so be prepared. Eliminating the cause may take even more time and work so get prepared for that, too. It's your job and the doctor can't do it for you, nor can any pill do the work for you.

Chemicals are used to grow larger quantities of food and there are over 10,000 additives in food to enhance the taste, appearance and preservation. Food is packaged and promoted. Fluoride in salt damages the pineal gland and has negative effects on human cognitive and physiological functions. It contributes to dementia[20] and it is a toxic waste by-product of the aluminum industry that boomed during World War II. Some researchers say that Nazi-led Germany was the first to introduce fluoride into the water supply with the supposed aim of curbing dissent in their population and in 1955, Proctor&Gamble's new brand, Crest, became the first producer of fluoridated toothpaste.[21] Many dentists are on record stating that dental caries are not caused by a lack of fluoride but rather by poor nutrition and the consumption of sugar. Many of the toxic chemicals used to enhance production, taste and appearance have a money motivation behind their use. It is my hope that we begin to use critical and creative thinking when it comes to the health care insurance industry or the food and drug administrations around the world, because they are not doing the jobs that they were hired to do. Who wants to make money from diseases through selling misinformation? Who wants to control us and our lives? Who are the people who present false information about what is healthy? Could they be pharmaceutical and health insurance corporations or the food and drug oversight committees? Please wake up.

Dr. Mercola's Nutritional Plan

Many today struggle with weight issues, diseases, and other health problems that impair their ability to enjoy life. Many resort to pharmaceutical drugs and other conventional methods to relieve their symptoms, but these are actually just Band-Aid solutions that typically result in more harm than good. What they don't realize is that they can significantly improve their health by just changing their diet and eating habits. Dr. Mercola's program

---

[20] Akinrinade, Memudu, Ogundele.*Fluoride and aluminium disturb neuronal morphology, transport functions, cholinesterase, lysosomal and cell cycle activities.* Pathophysiology. 2015

[21] https://www.britannica.com/topic/Colgate-Palmolive-Company

can help you achieve exactly that by adjusting your diet to center around high-quality fats.

Allopathic physicians, nutritionists, and public health experts have long claimed that dietary fat promotes heart disease and obesity. This deception caused people to follow low-fat, high-carb diets, which ruined the health of millions. Today, the general guideline for dietary fat intake is that it should only be 10 percent of your overall diet but Dr. Mercola prescribes that 50 to 75 percent of your daily calorie intake should be in the form of healthy fats.

The original food pyramid created by the U.S. Department of Agriculture (USDA) promotes a diet that has grains, pasta, and bread at its base (meaning they make up the majority of your diet) and fats at the top, or the smallest portion. But this can spell trouble, as grains break down into sugar in your body, driving up insulin and leptin resistance. Dr. Mercola's program, for instance, suggests that this food pyramid be flipped upside down and that everyone should be conscious of what they eat, avoiding processed foods that put our health at risk.

Introduction To Raw Politics

You can't eat oil or money. You eat food. Live enzymes in food are the key to good health. Cooking food denatures (modifies the molecular structure) it and diminishes its value. The organic farmers of the world are the seeds of the planet's future. They care about protecting the live enzymes without the use of poisons. Greed and the misuse of power and money destroy our individual hearts, collective humanity, and the planet. The heart is the center of our being and is nourished by love. The heart, spirit and soul work together to build a political consciousness. We are the grass roots of the world. We must connect in love and not be separated by fears, insecurities, differences or feelings of powerlessness. Our opportunity is here now, and the challenge that we face will strengthen us and keep our planet alive and vibrant. Help us build 'Raw Politics' by joining in our efforts to use the strength we have as leaders in love and vibrant health to reduce and eventually eliminate needless suffering.

In April 2007, the leadership of the *International Living Food Summit* issued a statement on the "optimum diet for health and longevity", returning to the ancient truth that the body heals itself when given the nutrients it needs. All the technology, funding, equipment, scientists, computer experts and politicians of the world cannot create a single seed. The power of nature is supreme. Our goal is to increase awareness that a happier, healthier humanity and planet is in the choices we make in our diet now.

As you read this, the human diet worldwide is controlled by the interests of multinational corporations, lobbyists, and other institutional giants looking to make a profit (and make us sick). The Food and Agriculture Organization of the United Nations and World Health Organization's Codex Guidelines For Vitamin and Mineral Food Supplements is trying to control how we get our nutrition. Raw Politics emphasizes a lifestyle of a more informed connection with our food through organic farming and eating a diet of fresh, raw foods intended to heal the body, the planet, and the social and political obstacles to peace.

The connection and relationship between a raw, organic diet and global politics may seem incomprehensible to many. Air, food, water and shelter are all necessary for humanity to survive, and raw, organic food has a relationship to each of these. Organic farming seeks to eliminate pollution, toxic chemicals and toxic building materials from its practice. The same number of acres used to grow food crops produces more food per acre than if that land were reserved for raising cattle. Preserved foods create waste from the paper (cartons), metal or glass that is needed for packaging. Waste produced by growing food crops is mostly compostable; unusable lettuce, root extensions from root vegetables, skins and peels can all be used again by any organic farmer.

Raw Politics will serve as the nucleus of a qualified group of visionary leaders whose lives are dedicated to developing a realistic path of actions to get to a healthier future. These actions will enhance the health of the planet and our inner and planetary peacefulness. They will foster responsible choices in thinking and behavior. Despair, hopelessness, powerlessness, and passivity will end and a planetary program for daily life choices will emerge that is in alignment with the laws of nature. Raw Politics will eliminate fear, greed, false, ego-based power, corruption, prejudice, irrational authority and the necessity to manipulate and control the world by asserting military, economic and political dominance in the name of democracy and freedom. Domination of other countries, including Ecuador, Indonesia, Iraq, Afghanistan, and others, whether by use of the World Bank or military brute force, will cease to be effective and will destroy the dominator in time.

When the old powers that be are ready to acknowledge that they are destroying none other than their own children and grandchildren, they too will begin to wake up to their short-sightedness and destructiveness. The Hegelian game of 'divide and conquer,' used for centuries to control humanity, will be revealed for the sinister trick of pitting one group of humans against another as a distraction from us seeing that they own both sides. They are distracting us from the increase of pollution, environmental destruction and disease that are the results of their greed and desire to control. Childhood cancer and diabetes, an increase in adult cancer, the genetic engineering of seeds and trees, global warming, the reduction of oxygen in the air and many other methods of destruction are the poisoned fruits of the insane, elitist behavior that believes that one small group of self-interested humans can put the lives and health of the rest of the planet in jeopardy to protect their continued gains.

Those who follow Raw Politics must realize they are the ones who need to emerge and lead this change from within the raw-food community. To those who are new to the raw lifestyle, we accept you and your food choices as you are. To achieve optimum health, we hope that you study and evaluate the benefits of a predominantly raw diet. The world needs your help to achieve sanity, the preservation and improvement of the planet and peace. Now is the time to cross boundaries, respect our slight differences, see the greater picture and organize and unite thousands of organizations, groups and individuals around the world. Using Raw

Politics as a foundation, melting pot, and grassroots organization, we will roll up our sleeves to create a new version of our future.

Why You Can't Lose Weight And Keep It Off

You already know the dangers of being overweight. But try as you might, you're still overweight. Maybe you've tried to lose weight so many times that you have given up. Diet pills and counting calories didn't work for you so you've accepted your fate. Most people need a 'wake up crisis' before they are ready to change.

Information about how to lose weight is available to anyone. Yes, there are so many different books and theories that it's hard to choose which one is right for you. But your trouble is that you read them and still delay in making any real or lasting changes to your lifestyle. You defend the way you live for your own contrived reasons and continue to go down the path of self-destruction, meal by meal, until the disease you are creating shows its head with a noticeable symptom. Can you tell when you have 500 cancer cells growing in your body? Not likely, since there is no proven way to find them until there has been enough growth to produce a noticeable symptom. Can you know when your colon is beginning to develop diverticula?

The key to losing weight starts in your mind, not in your diet. If you are willing to have a positive attitude and to open your mind, you can begin to understand what is preventing you from making changes in your choices. Change is very difficult because our habits are already formed and are repeated every day, making them stronger and more reinforced. The strength of our food habits and lifestyle can create a feeling of resignation in you, as though you are attempting the impossible task of changing the whole of who you are. Many of us actually give up and wait for the 'wake up crisis' to occur in the form of a heart attack, stroke, cancer, or diabetes.

You'll read this article and say "yeah, yeah, I know all that" and go on your way. Rather than increasing your awareness and consciousness, you choose to delay, procrastinate and avoid. Accepting responsibility for your health is a matter you've chosen to defer to your doctor. But how can you learn to face your weight if your doctor is overweight, too?

Dr. Jason Fung is one of the foremost experts in the world on fasting. He has gained insight into disease through his career as a Nephrologist (kidney specialist). Most kidney disease is linked to diabetes — and in order to get rid of the kidney problems, excess weight must first be managed. Dr. Fung discovered that fasting is much simpler than dieting and he uses it as a powerful tool to get his patients off diabetes medication and back to health. He recognizes that fasting reverses diabetes and prevents Alzheimer's, aging and cancer.

I recognize the good intentions of the many health care practitioners and their function to provide emergency and special treatment. However, I must also recognize the financial motivations of drugs, surgery, radiation, chemotherapy, certain tests and examinations, books, CDs, videos, hospital stays, the production line procedures of insurance companies and medical devices companies. Many contemporary surgeries cost over US$20,000, even though a doctor does not close a cut — the body does. All of the modalities have the potential to help and harm. Please do not forget that none of them heal or cure. Remove the cause and the body heals itself.

PART 3:

Holistic Integration

"It does not matter how slowly you go so long as you do not stop." —Confucius

THE FUTURE OF HEALTH CARE IS INTEGRATIVE

An introduction to Integrative Holistic Treatment

Integrative Holistic Treatment (IHT) is a clinical method involving the flexible, conscious combination of techniques from different therapeutic modalities based on the judgement of a health therapist. The goal of IHT is to help the patient, rather than to protect the therapist's investment in a particular therapeutic model. Using any therapeutic tool that is valid and appropriate in the moment enhances the treatment. The therapist experiences a sense of freedom regarding the choice of technique and a license to be creative at any given moment. The combination of these two elements stimulates a good feeling in the therapist and serves to solidify and enhance professional self-esteem. These feelings are often sensed by the patient and serve many constructive purposes in the therapy. For example, a patient may become hopeful upon sensing their therapist's feelings of competence and they may use the therapist's good feelings as a model for their own feelings.

When seen in the context of IHT, all health care theories are excellent tools for wellbeing. But when used in isolation, any modality will be limiting and will not always serve the complex needs of the patient. Using a single modality limits the understanding of the patient's symptoms. It predetermines the patient's needs as well as the therapist's response to those needs, rather than staying in touch with the ever-changing state of the patient. The patient is made to fit into the particular method rather than the therapist adapting their method to the patient.

IHT, by contrast, is a clinical approach that offers a practical, flexible and working method created intuitively by the therapist and suited to the individual needs of the patient. It draws upon many knowledge bases, rather than any single one. When one modality fails to overcome a health block, another modality can be introduced with fluidity. We need to remember that every theory serves as a guideline for thinking rather than the end thought in itself. The patient and the helping process must come before the ego and any one idea.

Integrative Holistic Treatment: The Foundation For Holistic Healing

Through the understanding and use of Integrative Holistic Treatment, the foundations for holistic healing can be formulated. As the integrative therapist adds new therapeutic modalities to their original studies, they develops a sense of the interrelationships between them. Gradually he expands his repertoire until a new dynamic core of theory and techniques begins to emerge. As that core grows with the addition of new information, a new entity begins to form, with a life of its own and its own energy systems.

The curiosity and challenge that emerges alongside the use of multiple modalities fosters the seeking of even more information. Each piece of new information is viewed as an important element of the whole, with a direct and meaningful relationship to the dynamic core. A certain inner frame of reference is established that fosters the acquisition of further new information. The core acts as a magnet, drawing in similar information. Connecting to new information is experienced as a "clicking-in" with the dynamic core, rather than as a piece of information from another modality that one is trying to relate to the original modality. The connection is an energetic one and the integrative therapist experiences it as a new and necessary piece of the whole core. As each new piece connects, the whole dynamic core grows and increases its capacity to attract more pieces. It is as though the core becomes a larger and more powerful magnet with the integration of each new piece. The old dynamic might temporarily lose its full potency, but the change that takes place facilitates a greater potency. Thus, the whole core reconstitutes and reorganizes itself, forming a new whole. In this holistic core reorganization, each element is truly integrated rather than being tacked on. This concept is the true foundation for holistic healing.

Holistic diagnosis is a prerequisite for holistic treatment. This may eventually be done by a holistic team led by open-minded, competent and non-competitive leaders. The team members will be sufficiently motivated and committed to this multi-dimensional diagnosis and ready to donate some of their time to learning. In IHT, the professional will be asked to put aside their personal and professional ego, as well as their competitiveness. They will be expected to have achieved sufficient personal maturity to be able to function productively in a loosely-structured situation under competent leadership. This holistic team, as with any group, will have a group process and dynamic, which in turn will be part of the diagnosis and interview process with the patient. The patient will need to be skillfully prepared for this examination, which is part of the healing process. The manner in which the pre-team initial examination is done would need to convey a positive attitude toward the patient and be sensitive to their needs. Giving appropriate information the the patient and assessing their fears, skepticism, cooperativeness, and general outlook is important. Respecting a patient's autonomy is necessary for them to be an active participant in their own healing process.

The composition of such a team may vary depending upon the availability of members. For example, one IHT team may include an allopathic doctor, a psychotherapist, a chiropractor, a Traditional Chinese Medicine practitioner, an ayurveda practitioner, a nutritionist, a polarity therapist, a rolfer, an acupuncturist, a Doctor of Osteopathy, and a Functional Medicine practitioner. The patient consultation procedure will evolve from a pre-examination team conference. This pre-examination information will be given to the IHT team leader who will assume responsibility for any immediate decisions. The team will seek to understand the causes of the patient's condition and how it brought about the formation of the symptoms. An evaluation of the patient's lifestyle is made so that the appropriate frame of reference can be developed. Assessing the patient's level of awareness of his condition, symptoms, lifestyle and sense of responsibility is important so that the type of patient participation can be gauged appropriately at the outset. Sudden changes are very rare, so appropriate goal setting is important.

Integration: A Revolution In Understanding The Body's Language

Integrative Holistic Treatment is about combining doctors and technology with more comprehensive knowledge and understanding. I first wrote about this concept in the 1970s in the hopes of appealing to psychotherapists to partner with physicians to treat the whole of the patient — mentally and physically. Today, are much more easily able to learn a lot about our own health and what is available to us to help us heal ourselves.

We are living in the information age but perhaps this has been in name only — until now. When it comes to medicine, information has been withheld from the professionals that are most adherent to the medical authorities in charge. Many of the world's alternative health care options have been in practice for long before the internet heightened their global exposure. But it is really only recently that allopathic practitioners have begun to learn alternative disciplines themselves. Their motivations may have had their foundations in capitalizing on the holistic "trends" growing in popularity; however, the pleasant side-effect is that they end up helping their patients with this additional health care knowledge.

Nevertheless, holistic health care practices are already emerging. These centers have a variety of professionals under the same roof, meaning that patients can obtain multiple services in one location. The important next step is for each of these professionals to open communication between each other about the health of their shared patients, and eventually, all patients in general. This discussion would be conducted without the professionals' egos and free from their individual financial motivations or political affiliations. And one giant goal is to allow space for the patient to be an active participant in the conversation. A donation of two hours of professional time per week is the basis for the starting model that we propose in this book. This may seem like a small step towards a lofty goal but it will be a significant milestone in the progress of health care that is currently lacking in almost all respects. It will offer a great deal towards improving the diagnostic treatment of the patient and the education of our health care providers as a whole.

Prevention

My personal idea of prevention is to be aware of and practice several steps in my daily decision making. The first step is to understand that how I think, feel and act are basic to the foundation of my health. I have made changes to my own life slowly, noticing a lack of knowledge and filling it as I go. I spent some time in a small village in the interior of Viti Levu (one of the Fijian Islands). There I realized that the basics for life were breathing, eating, drinking, and sleeping. The lives of the local villagers were almost that simple; they had one radio in the village, no TVs, no cell phones, no cars, and none of the other luxury amenities that many of us are accustomed to. Food was grown and harvested locally and I slept on a grass mat.

Currently, I live on a farm in Costa Rica. Here, I am able to concentrate on getting clean air, clean water, organic food, restful sleep and strengthening exercise, all of which lead to good health and emotions. Good food means living food grown in healthy soil that is naturally rich in nutrients without the use of chemical fertilizers. This quality of food is often referred to as *organic*. Although it can sometimes feel confusing when deciding *what* we should eat to keep our diet *clean*, luckily, nature provides us with fruit, vegetables, nuts and seeds, all of which are relatively easy to harvest when you live in a good climate for perennial growing. Food factories, on the other hand, create processed foods that are severely altered from their natural state of being, changing food into money by mass-producing unhealthy products. They devalue our natural food's nutritional content and focus on turning the resulting product into profit.

Good sleep means letting the body decide how much sleep it needs by going to bed early and following the laws of nature. This is the perfect time to meditate and allow the mind to become relaxed and naturally drift off to sleep. Staying away from screens before sleep will also help to prepare your mind for sleep.

Good emotions are necessary to our health, and include love, kindness and compassion. They inspire, motivate, and encourage responsibility. Negative emotions are those that are harmful to our health. They demean our intentions, hold us back, make us feel disappointed, angry and resentful, and destroy any care that we have for our health.

Good exercise means different things to different people. Learn about the different types of exercise, test them on your body, try different classes, and build up your personal routine over the years, progressing as you grow in experience. There's Tai Chi, yoga, resistance training, aerobics, various forms of martial arts, sports, walking, running, and so on. Each of them is beneficial in their own right.

The four main types of exercise are endurance activities, which increase your breathing and heart rate; strength exercises, which make your muscles stronger, balance exercises, which help prevent falls (a common problem in older adults); and flexibility exercises, which stretch your muscles and help your body stay limber. It doesn't matter how we get these four types of exercise as long as we get each type regularly. An ounce of prevention is worth a pound of cure.

Diagnosis

I have personally experienced and heard from others about health care practitioners who treat patients without making a thorough evaluation and diagnosis. This is especially true of allopathic health care practitioners who routinely prescribe pharmaceuticals as an automatic treatment to a patient's overt symptoms. These doctors practice medicine as though they are in a rush. Do you think they are motivated by money? I, myself, have been prescribed a spectrum of drugs by sixteen doctors, none of whom diagnosed the cause of my symptoms and many of whom did not even try. Some referred me for different diagnostic exams but none were able to diagnose the cause of my problems.

I tried allopathic and alternative practitioners, being prescribed Vitamin C infusions, hyperbaric chamber oxygen, homeopathics, herbal remedies, and even diet recommendations. It was my own research that led to my decision to visit a neurologist. He suggested that I take an MRI scan, after which I was diagnosed with a compressed spinal cord in my neck. New bone growth after an old injury was pressing on my spinal cord and causing pain and numbness in various parts of my face and body. I was getting progressively worse over seven years without a clue as to why. Seek the cause, get the proper diagnosis, and avoid rushing into the quick treatment of symptoms without understanding why they are there.

Dr. Joel Fuhrman, six-time New York Times bestseller and president of the Nutritional Research Foundation, specializes in disease prevention and reversing disease through nutritional methods. He practices functional medicine, which I suggest you study (there is a short chapter in the modalities section of the book that describes this practice). Dr. Furman believes that doctors are helpful in emergencies, accidents and burns, but that 90 percent of disease is caused by poor nutrition. He has determined that symptoms must be treated at this root cause of poor nutrition. Imagine, this is coming from a highly-recognized allopathic doctor! We are on the way to successful change to the integrative holistic concept.

Treatment

In holistic integrative therapy, treatment should come only after a proper diagnosis, except in some extreme emergency cases in which full diagnosis cannot be made quickly. At present, allopathic doctors decide most of their treatment plans according to their medical school education which can be limited in its scope especially when it comes to cutting-edge or ancient and alternative therapies. They are closed-minded because they are limited and they are limited because their professional egos convince them to stick to the treatments that they know.

When a health care practitioner wields only one tool, whether it be drugs, herbs, homeopathics, or anything else, they cannot claim to be practicing in the interest of the patient. They are professing to be experts in one thing, giving the patient a false sense of security that their diagnosis fits with the doctor's expertise. A doctor's confidence can make the patient's problem worse since the body is meant to heal itself. The doctor does not heal the body; however, rarely does a doctor understand or acknowledge this. In most cases, doctors do not want to understand and acknowledge their limited role because it would mean a loss of money and ego status.

Given the full extent of their diagnostic information, the patient should be actively involved in questioning their treatment. Patients should be encouraged to ask their doctor what are the side effects and long term effects are of their treatment. The drug, Omeprazol, is usually recommended for gastritis. I have been told to take it for a minimum of three months to start but the doctor never asked me what I eat regularly. Never did he mention that with certain food combinations, the drug can do significant damage to many internal organs. Over the last nine years that I have used my health insurance in Colombia, I have been prescribed at least forty different drugs. If I had took them all, even in succession, I might likely be dead by now.

A patient's lack of responsibility comes at a great cost to their health. This must be learned or there will be more disease-related deaths if patients remain passive and dependent on the current lucrative health care system that is based on treatment, not on prevention. The Holistic Integrative Treatment team is just the beginning step in a process of change. The team approach is meant to fortify the direction in which we are all going in our health. When professionals talk to each other, they gain a little respect and knowledge while taming their egos in the process. The concept of treatment that comes from the proper diagnosis of the patient's lifestyle, rather than from the point of view of selling pharmaceuticals or procedures. Treatment will become easier with a shift towards advocating responsible lifestyles, eliminating improper prescriptions, and doing away with our lazy attitude toward a patient's health education.

THE THEORY BEHIND INTEGRATIVE HOLISTIC HEALTH CARE

Holistic Solutions For Integrative Therapy

Learning discipline is the goal of many but it is only achieved by few. I mentioned my doctor friend before with the triple-bypass. He had the typical "crisis" mentality. Which do you have? The motivation to change, or the wait-and-see "crisis" mentality? Without discipline, goals will only be dreams. Some of us are disciplined when it comes to our survival needs. Others are disciplined when it comes to their ego, like the desire to be rich and famous. If you have already developed discipline in other areas of your life, you have the power to apply those same principles to your health! Use whatever discipline you already have! I chose to learn discipline because I wanted to prevent disease and slow down my aging process. I apply discipline in the physical, mental and emotional areas of my life. This enhances my spirituality. I am an 87 year old raw foodist who exercises 6 days a week. I'm not showing off — I'm trying to motivate you! Premature aging is a state that we are still learning to prevent. If we look at the lifespans of other mammals, they tend to live ten times the number of years that it takes them to reach maturity. Humans have a natural lifespan of up to 125 years[22], meaning that as a species we are still quite far from reaching our genetic potential.

---

[22] https://www.nature.com/articles/nature19793

You can fool everybody, but you can't fool your body. The choice is yours: prevention; or unnecessary disease, premature aging and loss of energy. Learning discipline is a process and you need to be motivated. Discipline starts with small achievable steps and slowly builds up with success at each step. Start when you are ready and do it on your own or seek support from professionals. Convince yourself that now is the time to start and take a small step in the direction of change every day. It really is that easy!

Self-Discipline And Prevention

How can we help ourselves and help each other?

The mind plays a crucial role in healing. The clinical application of the placebo effect proves that at least some small part of our minds is able to trick our bodies into healing. Many cancer patients today are opting to learn about the effects of diet, stress, lifestyle and more about their physical health. The cancer patients of yesterday felt helpless and submitted to radiation and chemotherapy without first considering making some changes in their lives.

As you read the following chapters, consider your own personal medical history — the illnesses you have had and how they were treated at the time. Practitioners and patients, ask yourselves: what would you have done differently in your treatment processes if you had had more information at the time? Think about the difference between treating the symptom of a disease and finding the root cause of a disease. What is the patient experiencing during their time with the practitioner? What psychological effects could treatment be having on them? Does the treatment contribute to the diagnosis? Which health care approach would you wish to try, or which combinations of modalities would you choose?

The Techniques Of Change

When you are ready, the following steps are suggestions for how to learn to accomplish change:

1. Self-observation — The observing ego (your outer eye, observing yourself from a distance) is used to locate the particular area in which change is desired or needed. This may be your fitness level, your diet, skin problems, aches, pains — anything that you *know* needs to change. For self-observation to take place, you will need to be motivated to look at yourself honestly. This is an easy thing to do when you are ready to look. No criticism is needed, only observation. For example, you may look at your level of physical fitness and ask whether daily exercise will enhance your condition. You may also look at your diet and desire to improve the quality and quantity of your food intake. Self-observation is the necessary first step that will affirm your intention to change and eventually help you set your goals.

2. Self-acceptance — Whatever exists is already accepted. By the very nature of your being, you belong here. Your experience is not wrong or incorrect but you can change it to change the course of your life. Negative or self-loathing attitudes are best left behind, because true acceptance of yourself is necessary to move forward. In order to change, you must accept that you are deserving of a positive future, no matter your past. Understanding the how and why of a particular situation in its historical roots is helpful if certain thought patterns keep recurring in your conscious mind. When the reasons for a thing are known, your rationality will assert itself and claim acceptance for what is, with an attitude set to move forward in a chosen, active direction. When self-acceptance is approached in this way, any negative or self-loathing attitudes will be attenuated by your reasoned intention.

3. Evaluation of your potential steps to change — After setting your intention to change, take inventory of what options are available to help you change. You may have a complex issue that you would like to tackle, such as one in which a thorough physical examination

will need to be made for muscle strength, endurance, cholesterol level, heart functioning, etc. An evaluation made in the area of diet may become an ongoing evaluation, as one becomes increasingly aware of more and new information. This is a step that will be ongoing, and will grow alongside your own progress on your path to change.

4. New goals are set — Setting new goals depends on the amount of information that you have taken in about your current situation. The amount of effort put into step 3 will determine how much change your goals will bring to your life. Gather your collected information when you are sufficiently motivated and then set more sophisticated goals and write them down into a step-by-step, daily plan. Use existing calendars, planners, apps — anything that will help you see your goals all day, every day.

5. Set limited goals to achieve the feeling of success — A limited goal is one that has guaranteed success. This step is used to achieve the big goals that you set in step 4. The goals must be so limited to begin that they are absolutely achievable. Every goal needs to be divided into its smallest sensible components. It is rare for anyone to make a radical change in old habits and maintain that change for the rest of your life. The goal of one hour of daily exercise can start with one minute of exercise, three times per week. If one minute is too long, reduce to thirty seconds. This small change is a key step. Here, a new habit is being formed through repetition. Three minutes of exercise a week is of vital importance to making a change to your fitness. Maintain this routine until it is done for several weeks to solidify your motivation to change.

6. Accept the slow rate of change — Recognize that the nature of growth is gradual, so setting your expectations high right from the start is not helpful. Following our example, if you suddenly jump from one minute to thirty minutes of exercise, the necessary inner processes (both physiological and emotional) will not have sufficient time to take place. Both our body and mind need to change in a gradual way in the same way that you did not gain weight overnight. Time is required for growth and patience is required from you to accept this slow rate of change. Accepting

this concept helps with the preparation for the road ahead, taking stock of your body and the new, small additions that you are adding to your goal. After one minute of daily exercise becomes easy to do, increase to two minutes or slightly more. This may take several weeks of one-minute time periods, until there occurs a desire or pushing from within to increase the time. This is an inner process unfolding, like a seed beginning to sprout. There will be an inner readiness and there will be a spontaneous desire that occurs. An important part of this concept is to stay in touch with yourself and to exercise your conscious will, too.

7. Find joy in the process — When change occurs from within, you will experience the process as an integral part of your growth. The combination of sustained effort and inner-readiness for change makes way for the next step forward. Each new step leads to the next one until the sub-goals are accomplished and finally the goal itself can be achieved. These accomplishments each bring a deep sense of satisfaction as each new sub-goal is accomplished. Observing your own gradual growth process taking place brings psychological rewards. Each new increase in time reinforces your prior sub-goal. Increasing from two to three minutes of exercise is both a statement of success and of continued growth. Maintaining the capacity of one minute of exercise is no longer questionable and your confidence is now being developed in real time. This confidence leads to the recognition of how this process can be applied to other areas of your life, thus becoming an integrated part of your personality.

8. Allow for regressions — During the course of change, regressions may occur. They must be accepted lightly and not be allowed to become destructive. After any regression occurs, repeat steps one to seven. We all need to allow for this natural part of the growth process called 'regression.' These are the times when life does not proceed according to plan. Regression may occur for various reasons and interrupt your steady progress. For example, feeling depressed, getting ill, or having an emergency may cause you to miss exercising one day. This is okay and will probably occur. Do

not put energy into missing a day — simply continue the program the next day.

9. Manage your thoughts — To do the above eight steps, it is important and necessary to realize that you must also change how you think. Our thoughts are able create feelings and emotions. The new thoughts that you are building will need to be connected to new feelings and new emotions. A helpful tool for building healthy connections between our thoughts, feelings and emotions is to remember that all of you is connected to your heart. Live as if the new behavior you want to achieve is already in motion so that you behave and act as if you are that change, experiencing the benefits of being in that new place. This concept is not new and comes from the Old Testament of The Bible, among other ancient schools of thought. Believe in yourself and practice doing what your new thoughts will enable you to do. As you practice, these thoughts will gain new strength until they manifest fully in your life. Don't repeat your old, debilitating thoughts anymore so as not to interfere with your process. If and when your old thoughts arrive, accept that they had their time and place and that you have moved on from there.

When these nine steps are applied, change will inevitably occur. As success in making a change is achieved, the capacity for making changes increases. Developing confidence both in the process and in yourself, it will become possible for you to experience greater personal freedom, unencumbered by doubt. With confidence in hand, there is no reason other than yourself to prevent you from developing more discipline, especially for your good health, your goals, and your life.

Alternatives To Taking The Personal Integration Path

There are three basic paths that allopathic medicine can take today. They are not all equal, so please review and consider how your personal choices align with these three paths:

Path #1: Doctors spend time learning awareness

Since the doctor will likely become the patient one day, doctors will be well advised to have the patience and honor to give at least one hour per week from their usual paid practice and dedicate that time to learning from other health professionals from varying practices and traditions. Every professional should recognize the limits of their practiced modality and learn that they do not know everything there is to know in their own profession; nor do they know everything about the health and wellbeing of the people they treat. The goal that we propose for healers of all kinds is to want to help each other — for free, which is a huge step for a financially-minded doctor. It's time for health care professionals to think of the future; to have a heart for their patients, and to want to cure the causes of disease, rather than focusing only on symptom treatment. Some doctors believe that they are in control of patients' health and well-being. These doctors need to gain distance from their egos and earn the perspective of self-observation.

Path #2: Insurance companies gain awareness

When allopathic doctors begin adopting alternative medicine into their daily practice, the health insurance companies will inevitably begin to lose money by not prescribing pharmaceutical drugs. If we work as a team and invite doctors who practice alternative medicine into insurance companies, this will secure the position of the insurance companies, who will now be serving a greater good.

Path #3: Governments gain awareness

The government will save taxpayer money when they align their health care support with more holistic values. Funds like Obamacare in the United States are suffering because of the huge strain put on it by a massively unhealthy population. The health of the people improves when the government supports programs that help people cure themselves, rather than mainly supporting the health insurance and pharmaceutical industries.

Interest Is Growing In Holistic Integrative Treatment

Dr. Daniel J. Benor, MD, suggests that there is a heightened interest in integrative care. It can be found in the blending of complementary/alternative medicine (CAM) with allopathic medical practice. This may be motivated by patients' demands for services that complement allopathic medical care, or it can also be motivated by a health care providers' awareness of economic opportunities. To a lesser, but growing, extent, integrative care is motivated by a health care provider's awareness of the benefits of complementary therapies.

Dr. Benor says:

"Wholistic approaches consider the person who has the illness rather than upon the illness the person has. Wholistic approaches empower patients to participate in their own health care. They enhance the integrity and the spirit of dignity in the healing encounter between careseekers and caregivers – who are increasingly under pressures of time and monetary constraints that are eroding their roles as caregivers. Complementary therapies introduce philosophies and methods of health care that promote whole-person care and acknowledge the place and needs of the caregiver in this process."

PART 4:

The Body Heals Itself

"Without health life is not life; it is
only a state of langour and suffering—
an image of death." —Buddha

You are a drop of rain
In this world so insane
As you fall through the sky
You make your soundless cry
The big river you fill
You feel the rushing thrill
Going down the fast stream
Just like your youthful dream
With your wild illusions
And your new confusions
And down and down you go
Part of the great big show
And then you disappear
And lose all your learned fear
You're part of the ocean
A big wave in motion
And then you vaporize
With no tears in your eyes
And in to the clouds go
To repeat the same show
You are a drop of rain
Forgetting all the pain
Dr. Walter J. Urban

MOTIVATION AND COOPERATION

With all the aforementioned in your mind, it is now up to you to understand and practice what will become the future of medicine. This is an *evolutionary* process, where resistance to learning and change exists, but as we can see, growth has already begun. The ideas presented in my 1978 book, <u>Integrative Therapy: Foundations of Holistic and Self Healing</u> prescribed this foundation for health care but they were premature for the mindset of the time period in which it was published.

Now, the seeds that were planted have begun to sprout.

Important Docu-Series On The Internet

There are a number of summits available online and in other video formats, all of which you can also attend live. The medium of the internet has allowed for the easy and inexpensive publishing and dissemination of inventive and innovative works. There is a growing list of health care practitioners and researchers who want to share new techniques that they have developed that cater to a community of people who are experiencing the same needs and sharing the same benefits.

Below is a short list of summits and documentaries series that have been streaming on the internet:

- The Sacred Plant
- Human Longevity
- Keto Edge Summit

- The Diabetes Summit
- Food Revolution Summit
- The Energy Blueprint
- Bible Health Secrets

These are crucial to know about and understand because they show the progress of our understanding and are a step in the direction towards global change. By sharing these summits for free first, these series producers show that they care about health first and making money second. Below are a few, select descriptions of three of the health summits currently online.

Beyond Chemo

Eighteen of the world's best cancer doctors and experts on the subject come together to reveal the safe, natural treatments that the $100 billion cancer industry doesn't want the public to know about. These experts discuss the safe, proven alternatives to chemo, radiation, and surgery in a free, 6-part video series.

The subjects tackled in <u>Beyond Chemo</u> include: how mainstream medicine profits from sickness, why the one-size-fits-all approach rarely works, and what alternative treatments do work.

Episode 1: Mike Adams, Dr. Paul Anderson, Dr. James Forsythe, and Dr. Patrick Quillin

- The TRUTH about the cancer industry. How they profit from sickness. And why they'll do anything to keep people from learning about alternative therapies
- Why "mainstream" treatments like chemotherapy, radiation, and surgery often aren't the best option, plus the alternative approaches
- The #1 step to take as soon as a patient receives diagnosis
- The dangers of "Betty Crocker" oncology and why mainstream medicine forces patients to take this approach (warning: this might tick off some Big Pharma execs)
- Episode 2: Dr. Josh Axe, Dr. Michael Murray, and Doug Kaufmann
- The true, root cause of cancer (it has nothing to do with genetics)

- How the FDA secretly poisoned the foods we eat and how these toxic chemicals silently cause cancer cells to grow at a rapid pace
- Why you MUST treat cancer like a fungus (THIS is why most mainstream treatments fail)
- A simple, dietary tweak that destroys cancer at the root (and how Dr. Josh Axe used this approach to help his mother overcome breast cancer)

Episode 3: Dr. James Forsythe, Dr. Paul Anderson and Dr. Frank Shallenberger

- The 3-part treatment that's 34X more effective than chemotherapy (is THIS the most powerful cancer treatment ever discovered?)
- How to starve cancer cells to death using Dr. Shallenberger's "Element 8" therapy
- A new way to treat cancer that's taking the medical industry by storm
- The exact approach Dr. Forsythe uses on his patients and how they have a 70% survival rate! (compare that to a 2% survival rate for conventional medicine)

Episode 4: Dr. Nasha Winters, Dr. Fred Pescatore, and Dr. Isaac Eliaz

- The shocking but true story of how Dr. Winters beat ovarian cancer on her own along with the exact protocol she uses to stay cancer free
- 7 supplements you MUST take if you want to send cancer into remission
- The #1 anti-cancer diet. Whether you recently had a diagnosis, or you're trying to prevent a recurrence
- A strange "fruit" which Dr. Isaac Eliaz uses with patients in his personal practice that has an 80% success rate in defeating cancer

Episode 5: Dr. Geo Espinosa and Dr. Lise Alschuler

- Dr. Espinosa's "CaPLESS" Method for defeating prostate cancer

- How Dr. Lise Alschuler overcame a breast cancer diagnosis and how she's kept cancer from coming back
- 1 simple "lifestyle hack" that's now scientifically proven to reduce your risk of breast cancer by 80%
- MEN: Is the PSA test a scam and which markers patients should look for instead

Episode 6: Dr. Nasha Winters, Dr. Lise Alschuler, and Dr. Frank Shallenberger

- 5 steps to prevent the "cancer comeback"
- Did you know 70% of survivors of certain cancers have a recurrence within 10 years?
- The exact anti-cancer protocol Dr. Shallenberger uses with his patients

Plant Fit Summit

This summit answers the important question of "what are the benefits of a plant-based lifestyle?" with testimony from experts like Dr. Michael Greger, Dr. Joel Fuhrman, Dr. Neal Barnard, Dr. Michelle McMacken, Olympic athlete Dotsie Bausch, Jeff Morgan and others. These health experts discuss how a simple act—like what we eat—can impact us on many levels. They suggest that it is through our diet that we can exude power over our health, wellbeing and life.

This summit covers all aspects of a healthy lifestyle in nutrition, fitness and mindset.

The Truth About Cancer: A Global Quest

Episode 1: The True History of Chemotherapy & The Pharmaceutical Monopoly

Episode 2: Cancer Facts and Fictions, Breast Cancer, Hormones, Skin Cancer & Essential Oils

Episode 3: Cancer-Killing Viruses, Cancer Stem Cells, GMOs, Juicing & Eating the Rainbow

Episode 4: Excitotoxins that Fuel Cancer, Nature's Pharmacy and Healing Cancer with Sound & Light

Episode 5: Cancer Causing Blindspots, Toxic Vaccines, Homeopathy & The Power of Emotions

Episode 6: The NOCEBO Effect, Healing Vaccines, Advanced Detoxing & Going Inside A German Cancer Clinic

Episode 7: Heal Cancer with Clean Electricity, Unique Water, Natural Sunlight & Combining Superfoods

Episode 8: Cannabis, Nature's Epigenetic Switches, Peptides & Healing with Micronutrient Therapy

Episode 9: Cancer Conquerors & Their Powerful Stories of Victory

Healing Power Of Food Summit

"Food has always been magical to me. It nourishes. Heals. Comforts. Inspires, and brings us joy throughout our lives. There's nothing else that has this kind of power.

"Even after a lifetime of studying food and nutrition, I am still awed by the inherent magic of nature and the food she gives us. If you think about it, food is our direct connection to nature. It interacts with our bodies in complex and seemingly miraculous ways.

"It plays a major role in the composition of the cells throughout our bodies and influences how we function, think and even how we feel.

"Now a new era of food awareness is emerging; people are concerned as much about healthfulness and diversity of foods as they are about flavor.

"With the epidemic of obesity, diabetes, cancer, and other diet-related diseases exploding, worldwide, improvements in the quality of food we eat cannot happen soon enough."

— Dr. Michael Murray

Holistic Wellness Centers

In addition to online health summits, holistic wellness centers are beginning on the path of integrative therapy by joining together multiple modalities under one roof. Below are two examples of incredible health care work being done to bring together many therapies for the holistic healing of patients.

Live Young Sky Lakes Wellness Center

The mission for the Live Young Sky Lakes Wellness Center in Klamath Falls, Oregon, is to empower everyone to live a healthier life by practicing preventive medicine. They attempt to demonstrate a more effective health care model that strengthens health and wellbeing through chronic disease prevention and reversal, community policy, and innovation.

The center's values include:

1. Approaching health care differently by creating unique and innovative solutions through multidisciplinary efforts.
2. Empowering patients and community.
3. Providing a safe environment free from judgment, prejudice, bias and stigma.
4. Providing access to the Wellness Center services to all.
5. Creating positive change within the community.

Practicing a lifestyle of making mindful choices while improving quality of life and well being are the the primary focus of the services offered at Sky Lakes. After successfully offering wellness programs to Sky Lakes employees and their spouses, the center expanded to offering its services to the general public.

Staff offer participants classes in stress management and/or weight loss, as well as courses in mindful meals and healthy cooking. Individuals meet one-on-one throughout the year for classes, attend one-on-one visits with a dietician and a physician, and receive other health updates. All programs are focused on personalized preventative care instead of a strictly reactive approach.

The staff at Sky Lakes hope that insurance companies can at some point cover the cost of their services. They encourage all patients to approach their insurance companies to see if they will be willing to reimburse. For now, the clinic is self-pay only.

Southampton Hospital's Ed & Phyllis Davis Wellness Institute

The Ed & Phyllis Davis Wellness Institute was formed several years ago to use mind/body medicine to promote health and wellbeing in their patients. Their clinicians provide patients with an integrative approach to medicine, empowering them to be proactive in their own health management by offering a wide variety of services and classes to help patients cope with their illness. They likewise offer their services to healthy patients who want to continue living a healthy lifestyle.

This wellness institute acknowledges that stress has a negative impact on the immune system. By controlling stress, they believe that the body is better prepared to heal and react to standard medicine. They believe that leading a healthy lifestyle is a central part for managing disease and keeping patients healthy. Their functional medicine program focuses on preventing disease rather than treating existing symptoms. By taking a comprehensive look at the patient, their functional medicine doctors are able to evaluate what threats a patient might face in the future, and managing their currently existing problems.

Program Manager Jessica Swiatocha says that "when you go to the doctor's office, they're able to give you a prescription, but we're looking at doing the other portion, and making you feel completely whole — not just fixing part of the problem."

The Institute makes use a variety of treatments, services and therapies to help patients deal with their specific needs, including massage therapy, nutritional counseling, acupuncture, hypnotherapy, biofeedback, personal training, yoga, Pilates, Tai-Chi, art therapy, meditation, and much more. They also offer programs that help patients manage weight loss, Parkinson's disease, breast cancer, cardiac disease, and diabetes among others.

Swiatocha says, "I feel strongly that the future of medicine is integrative medicine, and that having a patient become a proactive part of their health care and be a participant instead of being told to take this or take that is what people are looking for now."

Socrates Wellness Institute In Costa Rica

Socrates Wellness Institute provides patients with a hands-on experience in implementing life changes to overcome all disease and sickness, and to use the knowledge gained to preserve this state of wellness for a lifetime.

The leaders of this institute categorically deny any ability to heal any disease. They instead offer their skills to teach you how to heal yourself. They recognize that the only healer is your own body.

Their intense program of immersion takes a participant into all aspects of wellness. They teach the skills to continue on healing and to reach a state of total wellness with the ability to sustain it for a lifetime. Socrates Wellness Institute decries the use of drugs, surgeries, radiation or chemotherapy treatments. As a child of Mother Nature, our path to wellness is based solely on all-natural elements exactly as they are provided in abundance by Nature herself. Participants take back home a re-introduction to what they already know deep inside their 'higher being'. They teach a state of awareness that has been suppressed or forgotten by a system that makes billions of dollars in profit from selling pills and injections. The Socrates wellness method, on the other hand, is a learned lifestyle and totally effective.

Socrates Wellness is different because determining the root causes to problems requires a comprehensive analysis of many factors, requiring considerable time for discovery and correlation. To rectify this root cause and bring the body/mind/spirit complex back to homeostasis, Socrates Wellness Institute prescribes adopting lifestyle changes that help the person to return to its natural state of balance. In other words, disease always stems from lifestyle issues that force the complex into a state of energetic imbalance, an unnatural state, that will heal itself when conditions allow. No one can heal another. The body/mind/spirit complex can and will heal itself.

THE MIND, EMOTIONS, AND THE ROLE OF STRESS

"Emotions are humanity's motivator and its omnipresent guide." — Thomas Lewis

We know that the body possesses its own intelligence. It heals itself without the need for our conscious mind's interactions, as can be observed in the closing of a cut. This *body intelligence* can be used for self-healing when you learn to speak your body's language with your conscious mind. The body tells the mind when something goes wrong. The mind tells the body's own "intelligence" to energize the blood cells, clean the cut and ease the pain quickly, speeding up the circulation in the pain area and clearing away the wastes in the form of a scab.

Tune into your body intelligence. Take the time to tune into it as you eliminate what no longer serves you in pursuit of your goals. Become aware of where you have discomfort. Pinpoint the exact area and intensity of the discomfort. Consider what might be the cause or causes of your discomfort. Focus the mind on healing and invite the cooperation of your mind, body and spirit. Expect discomfort or pain to arrive in due time, and use the mind, body and spirit to unite in healing intention, with directive coming from the conscious mind.

The body can and does heal itself. It wants to maintain itself and to have good health. It knows that it needs good nutrition and the elimination of all sources of toxins. Your knowledge of this goes back to your mother's health condition when pregnant. Eating whole, live, natural foods is crucial to give the body the nutrition it needs, and to transfer that knowledge of what it feels like to eat healthfully to your children. Eliminating what harms the body is the other half of the process. Both lessons are important to harvest for yourself, and to pass on in your family's genetic body intelligence.

The Mind's Role In Health

Our whole beings are composed of body, mind, and spirit, and the interactions between them. Civilization, too, is bound to advance as we work together. Working together to learn from nature and from each other is the cornerstone of the future of healing — both our individual selves and the planet.

The idea of good health can be as simple as giving the body, mind, and spirit what they need, while removing what they don't need, to function optimally. As research advances, the needs of the body are better understood. This is especially so for the body's nutritional needs. Current research pertaining to the body's nutritional needs is focused on defining the right kinds of fats.

But we must go beyond the body's needs and also pay attention to our need for finding or creating a healing environment in the mind, and specifically our emotions and feelings. A toxic relationship may be the main impediment to your digestion of good nutrition because the negative actions in the relationship spur on negative emotions that breed negative feelings in the person. Antonio D'Amasio, professor of neuroscience at The University of California and author of several books on the subject, explains it as: "Feelings are mental experiences of body states, which arise as the brain interprets emotions, themselves physical states arising from the body's responses to external stimuli. (The order of such events is: I am threatened, experience fear, and feel horror.)"

Dr. Bruce Lipton, author of <u>The Biology Of Belief: Unleashing The Power Of Consciousness, Matter And Miracles</u> (2005), talks about thoughts as forms of energy capable of movement and action. The strength of the thought is directly matched by the strength of the will. Practicing mind control allows us to select our thoughts and control our lives. If we are able to eliminate negative thoughts from our minds, we can have the energy to concentrate on what is good for us. When you pull the weeds from your garden, the good seeds have the room to grow. In this seminal book on the power of the mind, Dr. Lipton describes in detail how thoughts can affect the cells in our bodies. The proper functioning of the cells is the foundation of good health. Our thoughts, both conscious and unconscious, affect the body. The mind can become a powerful tool for health and all thoughts are important to consider in the analysis of health.

Some scientists have theorized that DNA can be reprogrammed by words and frequencies. Our minds are not separated from our bodies, organs and individual cells. Each of these units are affected by love, thoughts and emotions. Approaching each of these units with compassion serves to build trust between them. Make friends with your body and ask it to help you with what you want to accomplish. Different thoughts will release different hormones in your body, so be clear and deliberate with your communications with your body: talk to your cells, clear the debilitating memories and plant new, positive thoughts.

The Strength Of The Mind

From early in life, we are exposed to ideas, beliefs, images, symbols and more, that teach us our values. These experiences shape what we think, what we do and they affect our health. As we are exposed to the masters of mind control, like our world's mega-corporations and mainstream media, we are told how and what to see, think, do, and feel. In effect, we are conditioned to obey. We receive direct suggestion and subliminal messages from corporations every day and we are pressured to comply with their will.

We have all become the victims of a grand system of oppression, most of us without knowing that it is occurring. We are conditioned to respond automatically. Very rarely are we encouraged to think critically or to view ourselves from a distance so that we do not notice our conditioned state. There is little nourishment for our imaginations or our creativity in the main streams of society. This is our reality because those in charge want to stay in charge (a false system that is often referred to as 'The Matrix').

All of this applies to health and disease because our so-called "health care" systems around the world have developed into lucrative insurance businesses for which our diseases are the assets. This has begun to change in the recent decades of growing consumer awareness, where the concept of disease prevention has become a bigger priority for more people. Many are choosing to avoid becoming patients in the first place. This change will be beneficial for all but the old medical insurance models, which currently continue to dominate. The Federal Drug Administration in the United States relies on fees and payments from pharmaceutical companies, whose products the agency is tasked to regulate. This type of system cannot elicit fair or accurate results about the safety or efficacy of the drugs it "regulates". For example, recently GlaxoSmithKline's diabetes drug, Avandia, was linked to thousands of heart attacks[23]; and Paxil, an antidepressant, was discovered to exacerbate the risk of suicide in young

---

[23] https://www.reuters.com/article/us-glaxosmithkline-avandia/glaxos-diabetes-drug-may-cause-heart-attacks-idUSL2170925720070522

people[24]. Another pharmaceutical manufacturer, Merck, has a pain killer called Vioxx that was linked to thousands of heart disease deaths[25].

We are all challenged to change. Change is needed from the doctor and the patient. Both need to realize the interdependence of all different types of medicine, which all have their individual effects that hold value in the healing process. Both doctor and patient are responsible for bringing together the integrative holistic team, remembering to do their research and choose the practices that have the biggest benefit to our health. In his more recent book, The Wisdom of Your Cells: How Your Beliefs Control Your Biology (2006), Dr. Bruce Lipton discusses the effects that the mind can have on a cell. For a medical practitioner to have an open mind, free from fear and focused on the primary goal of helping their patients, the practitioner must overcome their fears and leave their ego at home. They must learn to work for the good of the cell; their community of patients and practitioners.

We realize that having an open mind to learning new modalities may affect the practitioner's self-image and status in society. In fact, the medical elite's self-image, status, financial success, and their need to feel superior, have been the drivers of some of our scientific development in the field of health, such as the development of MRI technology. But the strength of our minds is in our flexibility and ability to accept how we got here, while also changing the direction in which we want to go.

Yes, You Are Safe

When you have fear, you don't feel safe. Fear is the great obstacle in life. Some people live with conscious fears of the endangerment of their lives, and those of which they love. Many more are burdened by unconscious fears acquired early in life from overwhelming situations. If left undisturbed, these unconscious fears remained buried in you for your whole life and

---

[24] https://www.nytimes.com/2015/09/17/health/antidepressant-paxil-is-unsafe-for-teenagers-new-analysis-says.html

[25] http://www.nbcnews.com/id/6192603/ns/health-arthritis/t/report-vioxx-linked-thousands-deaths/

affect your thoughts, actions and health, without your conscious awareness of the root cause. Fear may prevent you from achieving your life's purpose or specific goals; and it may prevent you from loving and being loved.

Life is filled with situations that are constantly changing. How you react to external change is determined by your life history. If you accept the history that you are given through your genes and your passive or childhood experiences as your ultimate truth, you will be likely to avoid change. But if you accept your history as such and still work to change, you will in essence be rewriting history with new footnotes to how your past helped you change.

Many react automatically due to the established neurochemical pathways that keep repeating over and over again. Learning how to free yourself from these reactions is important for your future. If they control you, your freedom is diminished or lost. Your life becomes limited by your lack of information. Many people are unaware that they are living in a self-limiting world and keep repeating what they have always done. It's like living in a self-created "jail" without realizing you are there. You have accepted that you have no choice but to live in that jail because of your life history. But with the right awareness and motivation, you can free yourself. You may need help because the unconscious is not easily accessible. If you don't succeed on your own, seek out professional help, as you would with a dentist or a car mechanic. You can overcome all your fears and feel safe and free—you just have to get out there and do it.

Mental Techniques For Change

1. Search and become aware of your ideas, thoughts, beliefs.
2. Evaluate learned ideas of past environment.
3. Eliminate what is not useful now.
4. Eliminate negative thoughts, feelings, and emotions.
5. Develop new ideas about self and world.
6. Keep ego in check through self-observation.
7. Commit self to self cultivation by positive thoughts, speech, and actions.

8. Practice understanding and compassion for all people and life on this planet.

9. Believe in yourself; your inner strength, life force and self-love.

10. Never give up.

11. Control your thoughts.

12. Get yourself unstuck and free your mind.

13. Daily study and practice of how to achieve your goals.

14. Make commitments to yourself.

15. Develop more discipline.

16. Allow your thoughts to flow freely sometimes and observe where they go.

17. Think about your body; scan it mentally to see if there is discomfort or pain anywhere.

18. Never blame anyone or anything.

19. Take complete responsibility for your life and be your own doctor and psychologist (within reasonable limits).

20. Think before you speak, and when possible, and learn to listen with patience and compassion, especially when you disagree.

21. Never forget to love yourself and others.

22. Realize that the only limits you have are those you put on yourself.

23. Realize that you are limitless in your potential to develop yourself.

24. Cultivate your mind with new studies, maintain self-confidence, and be persistent with great endurance.

25. Always remember that you are in charge of your thoughts.

The Need To Prevent Stress And De-Stress

Never in my life has a doctor asked me about the role of stress in my life. This is astonishing to me since it is a well known fact of modern medicine that stress affects health in many ways. Throughout our lives, we experience physical stress from environmental challenges, such as by breathing in too many chemicals. Some of the common feelings associated with physical stress are fear, guilt, insecurity, pressure leading to pain, and inability to cope.

Freud wrote about the fight or flight response pertaining to stress. A stressed person will experience bodily reactions like a rise in blood pressure and heart rate, muscle tension, etc. Some of us have food cravings, some turn to drugs. Others do reckless things with their bodies. Gaining and maintaining control of your physical reactions to stress is achievable with disciplined exercise, meditation, yoga and more are healthy ways to cope with stress.

Emotional reactions to stress can be anger, helplessness, frustration and restlessness. But there are also symptoms of stress that are useful tools for a person who is focused, alert and able to mobilize their body's energy. Perform a self-examination about your stress levels regarding the different parts of your life. Are you stressed physically, mentally, or emotionally? Control and discipline can prevent stress and mitigate existing stress levels.

You may also be subject to unconscious stress, such as from an old memory of when you were frightened as a child. When you hold on to stress for long periods of time, you accumulate a load of withheld emotions that may set off a larger reaction. For example, anger that has been withheld over a period of time may be set off at any time by a small trigger that can lead to an explosive reaction. It is believed that anger affects the liver. According to Traditional Chinese Medicine, sadness is believed to be associated with an imbalance in the lung and large intestine system. The creation of electrical imbalances in the body is thought to be responsible for these correlations and it is critical to your health to release negative memories stored in your cells, and especially before they are stored.

The Road To Freedom: Eliminating Stress, Fear And Negative Emotions

There are many roads to freedom. To be free is to not be limited by yourself or your environment. To be true to yourself and to who and what you really are is to discover your innermost being is free. We each attain different degrees of freedom in our lives because we all are limited by our life history. There are many limiting factors that interfere for each of us, including stress, fear and negative emotion. Most of us are aware of our stress and many of our negative emotions. But we tend to deny our fears and often they are unconscious. We cannot eliminate what we are not aware of; so to eliminate fear, it must be made conscious.

Fear is what I call a "bottom line" emotion. Fear usually develops when we perceive a threat and then feel powerless. Many fears begin in childhood and are suppressed or repressed with age. Repressing fears means moving them from your conscious mind to your unconscious mind. Suppressed fears are pushed away and still in our consciousness. Any average person may be able to say that they have no fears, but solely because they are not aware of them. In my work as a psychoanalyst and psychotherapist, I have found that a great many things boil down to fear, whether conscious or unconscious. When a fear becomes conscious, it can be experienced and dealt with on a rational, adult level. The elimination of fear is therefore possible… when it is discovered.

In my book, <u>Do You Have The Courage to Change</u> (2004), I describe the many ways that people can manifest repressed emotions and the patterns of behavior that they unconsciously create. Many people do not want to experience their buried fears, for example, because of the pain involved in re-experiencing them. To repress these fears is denial. In denial there may be some consciousness of the fear but it is easily denied as a way of protecting against a more immediate, painful, emotional experience. Repressed fears usually require professional help for most people to find, accept and cope. You can begin by reading <u>Courage to Change</u> and try out some of the exercises that I suggest to help patients overcome their repressed emotions.

Honesty with yourself is a tool to work on in the elimination of conscious fears. Many conscious fears can be dealt with in a rational manner if there is enough air, food, water, sleep and shelter available to the person who wants to face their fears. If you are faced with bullets, bombs, earthquakes, or any other danger, it is likely that you will be too overwhelmed to face any other conscious fears that you have stored inside you. The most immediate fears will always dominate our conscious minds.

In my work I often get to a person's fears rather quickly as it is an important basic issue for almost everyone. Fear interferes with the capacity to love, which is a tool in any healing process. Negative emotions and ideas like fear, anger, worry, doubt, depression, guilt, anxiety, panic, etc. are also contributors to stress and disease. Emotional reactions become habits that are consistently reinforced by the same stimuli. Our very own beliefs and ideas may cause us to react to ourselves and stimulate negative emotions. Sending positive messages to your body will enhance your ability to change. One of the major joys of life is the capacity to love and have compassion for others. This becomes more and more possible when we eliminate stress, fear, and negative emotions. We need to nourish our hope so that the body and mind can heal itself when you know what you need to do. The road to freedom is available to all of us. Just take the first step and you are on your way to love and a better life.

Emotional Resonance

Emotions have many names: love, joy, serenity, ecstasy, anger, rage, annoyance, disgust, boredom, surprise, anticipation, fear, panic, and anxiety. They may be divided into categories of positive and negative emotions, as they typically are. Whether they are "positive" or "negative," they affect our health.

According to Traditional Chinese Medicine, our emotions affect each of the organs in our bodies in different ways. Emotions affect our ability to think clearly and logically. They are what keep us different from androids, which cannot be made to reproduce genuine emotions. Masking our emotions helps us to avoid facing issues that we don't want to face. But pushing them into the unconscious can contribute to disease by affecting the flow of energy in our body. Numerous different modalities point to these energy blockages as an important contributor to disease.

Emotions and feelings can be considered to be different. "I feel tired and am angry." 'Tired' is the feeling and 'anger' is the emotion. Feelings (like tired, hungry, pain, bloating, etc) refer to the body's physical reactions.

Your mind is in control of your emotions. Emotions come from your interactions with your inner world and feelings come from your interactions with your body and the external world.

Emotional pain can cause physical, *feeling* pain. Since most people fear death, let's use this as an example. Fear is an emotion, and depending on how you think of death, your level of fear may be high or low. To simplify the options of what happens at death, let's say that no knows if our spirits live on, or if they disappear into oblivion. But how you react to this fear is your responsibility regardless. You may either face desperation, which leads to stress, which will likely lead to physical manifestations of your internal, emotional pain; or you may gain control over your emotional response and say: "I will face death, accept it, let go of my fear, and move on with my life."

When you look at what makes you feel emotional, you will see that there are some reactions that come and go, and others than linger for a while and even cause physical sensations. When we properly analyze feelings and emotions, we see that they are not separate in their effects — they are merely categorized by how we are affected by their presence in our individual lives.

Analyze what makes you feel frustrated, angry, sad, happy, depressed, and try to learn about the situation so you don't continue to repeat your negative emotional reactions. Love and compassion are the healing emotions to have, and those that lead to stress are the ones to dispel from your life.

For me, where I am in my life right now, I am grateful for whatever emotions I experience, and I say "thank you" to myself for being alive in every moment.

Create Courage, Not Fear

Let go of fear and the security of the economic and social nest you have built and fly somewhere new to strengthen your wings. Fear is the most typical base line emotion for the harmful emotions like doubt, worry, anxiety, and frustration. The root cause for fear is a sense of powerlessness that stems from some moment in your life history. These 'events from the past' were so overwhelming for you that a feeling of weakness and powerlessness developed in you. When you uncover, understand, and properly treat these events and look at them with the freshness of the current moment, they can be put into a helpful or help-prepared perspective. When this is done, a new freedom is born out of which you can and will develop courage. Every moment in each of our lives is a teacher to those of us who have developed sufficient awareness and consciousness. Life's experiences can be a source for courage. Something that was frightening in the past can become the stimulating challenge needed to develop courage. Every fear that we challenge becomes another opportunity for personal development.

Welcome fear as your teacher and you will become more capable of mentally conquering any personal challenge that you have to face. When you are motivated to make the choice to accept fear as your teacher, life will become a more exciting adventure. When you create more courage in our world to stand up for what is good and helpful, you will be rewarded with new growth of inner strength. An example can be as simple as saying something you were afraid to say even though you knew that you should; or taking a trip by yourself to a foreign country where you don't speak the language as an opportunity to explore a new culture and grow in your ability to connect with a new people.

Living with greater courage is its own reward. Facing the challenge of the economic and political crisis in the world brings a great opportunity for growing courage inside each of us. Now is the time to learn that you are not powerless by facing your fear of the unknown and diving in deep, learning everything that you can about how to help yourself and the world around you. We know that we can do it; and you can do it, too!

Changing Fear Into Love

Franklin D. Roosevelt said "there is nothing to fear but fear itself." I consider this statement to be half-correct. Yes, there is nothing to fear, and we don't need to fear "fear itself," either.

What causes fear? What is behind fear? When you investigates why there is fear in your life, what is the situation that made you feel the most powerless? I gave a lecture at a workshop where I asked the participants how many have fears. I was surprised that almost everyone raised their hands. Fears originate from the past, present or thinking about the future. They can be internally or externally caused. As children, we may develop fears due to forces that we cannot control and these forces of various kinds may continue having an effect in adolescent and adult life.

Fears may also be buried deeply in our personality and not show up under ordinary conditions, but can manifest in times of great stress. Unconscious fears need more work to be discovered. Conscious fears tend to be easier to work with. Both are equally dangerous to health. When one is raised with feelings of love, self-worth and self-esteem, their foundation for dealing with fear is much stronger and they are therefore less likely to manifest the fearful feelings of worry, self-doubt, a sense of inadequacy or a feeling of being unlovable.

The first step to face your fear is to own the fear rather than deny it. Bringing the fear out into the open and clearly understanding it begins with looking as its history and tracing back to its origin. Many fears are made stronger by repetition, thus requiring more work to get to the source.

Fears that come from an external threat are more easily understood than internal threats. The fear of losing your job or your mate may be the trigger mechanism that leads you to manifest a larger 'reality fear,' like that of being homeless and without food. External fears can become internal fears, such as the fear of being lonely, isolated and unworthy. Fears can be both external and internal. Internal ones are fears created in the mind. External fears come to us from outside of ourselves.

Every person, as a unique individual, has his own perceptions of the same situation as well as his own individual reactions that are influenced by his life history. But as mentioned before, the ultimate fear for many is the fear of death. So far, it appears that we all must die. Some believe that our spirit lives on forever and that the energy from our being returns to another form or even into its original form.

Regardless what you believe about life after death, if we come to terms with death, at least the death of our bodies, before we actually die, we can eliminate this fear from our present life. Everyone handles things differently, but the best way that I can describe this is that it happens by changing fear into love.

Changing fear into love depends on your beliefs and your personal place in your community, both local and global. A Haitian eating mud pies sees the world very differently than the CEO of Intel or Goldman Sachs. A Nigerian oil worker, an Israeli soldier, an Indian farmer, and the Indian farmer's neighbor may each have a very different living environment that induces different psychological makeups and beliefs. But they do all have one thing in common: the instinct to survive. This instinct can, of course, be overcome by years of submission to devout beliefs that foster suicidal actions, like with a suicide bomber or anyone in the military. We will ignore these people for the purpose of this book because their situation requires much more detailed work. For the rest of us, the desire to live has created various types of adaptations. The rest of us can see that there is always another solution that we can pursue.

Changing one's belief system is a big job. We are frequently unaware of the full extent of our belief system until is it made conscious through self-reflection. Doing this takes investigative work and often requires help. When all beliefs are made conscious and fully understood in their origins and history, they can be critically evaluated. After that, choices can be made as to which beliefs are of current value, which can be modified and which can be eliminated.

Revising beliefs can have great influence on the process of change. Even just entertaining new beliefs in your mind can influence your thoughts, emotions and actions. New beliefs based on new information allow for more responsible choices, where more considerations are felt and understood. Feelings of powerlessness and threats can be reduced and even overcome when we see that there are more ways to think of a scenario. Understanding that your internal threats may be based on childhood fears will allow you to use a more logical, adult perception and reaction to a situation. For example, a powerless child facing an angry parent can now be perceived quite differently from the perspective of a logical, independent adult, and an adult's understanding of the expressions of a parent's emotions can lead to the development of more patience. Cultivating patience can lead to self-discipline. Growth leads to freedom, then to forgiveness, which brings you to the freeing feelings of love, gratitude, and joy.

Love is something that is felt and given. A bell only works when you ring it, and it is only the action of ringing the bell that makes the bell what it is. Let this one small example serve as your ideal for changing fear into love. Taoism explains that everything is part of the Great Way. Costa Ricans have the saying, "pura vida," which directly translates to "pure life" but more accurately translates to mean "whatever happens is part of life." Threat to life is a reality. The question now becomes, "how do you react to threat?" If you are in charge of your reactions, know enough about different possible reactions, and you are able to choose how to react, you may be able to perceive the threat, even of death, in a different way. With enough reinforcement through practicing a fearless belief system, fear can eventually be eliminated. The Samurai had the saying, "today is a good day to die." Though no one wants to die, when we live a life that we are happy with, today can be as good as any other day to die because life simply cannot get any better when we feel love rather than fear.

Life threatening forces may come from humans or from nature, but it is the path to disease and death that is surely the more harmful state of affairs. Those humans who have inflicted death or slow death through pollution, contamination, and disease creation are part of the world we live in, and yet we are often advised to "turn the other cheek" and to learn forgiveness. Once again, this is easier said than done. How can we turn fear into love in some of the most horrible scenarios created by the most malicious parts of humanity? Can we ever do it? Can we control what seem to be automatic psychological, emotional and physical reactions? Can understanding lead to forgiveness? Can you really free yourself from your reactions?

We face many external threats in our newly global paradigm, with its unemployment, foreclosures, national debts, interest rates and many other situations that arise due to free market greed. We feel these threats implicitly. How do we react to these threats? We can react either with fear, or with calm thinking founded in a belief system that allows us to get enough perspective of the bigger picture. What was hidden must be placed clearly in the open so it can be cleansed. This entire process depends on what you believe. Do you have spiritual awareness? Do you understand or believe that all is vibrations of light energy that transforms rather than dies? If this has made you think a bit or even motivated to study, I am delighted!

Control Your Emotions

A fundamental problem between couples is that there is a lack of emotional control. Without emotional control, effective communication can't take place. Without adequate two-way communication, problems are almost impossible to solve. Unsolved problems lead to the breakdown of the relationship, which may lead to the ending of the relationship, or even to violence at times as an alternate outlet. There is a difference between feeling emotions and expressing them in an appropriate way and feeling them and letting them take over without any sense of control.

A frequent runaway emotion is anger. Anger may be felt and expressed helpfully by saying something like: "I feel angry when you spend more money than we can afford." Shouting in anger and saying something like: "you spend too damn much money!" is unhelpful and likely to provoke a response that is not going to solve the situation, potentially escalating the anger of those involved. Those who give into anger develop secondary problems such as withdrawal or coldness towards others.

Lacking emotional control means that a person skews towards being reactive rather than reflective. Some people have quick, almost automatic responses. They have been conditioned to feel like they have no other options but to react. A reactionary disposition (which can be positive or negative) is typically developed in early life after being exposed to reactionary role models and having these responses reinforced through constant, sometimes daily repetition. With each repetition, the response becomes more automatic and harder to recognize as outside of the self, therefore difficult to change. Very often, a person is not aware of how automatic their reactions are and when pointed out to them, they may become defensive. They do not recognize that part of themselves as capable of change. Ask yourself: who is in charge of your emotions? Are you satisfied with your emotional reactions? Do your reactions interfere with the kind of relationships you want to have?

If you want better relationships you must take the responsibility for your self-observation, self-evaluation and your decision to change. Emotions can create physical changes in your body; for instance, anger can damage your liver over time, anxiety and fear can reduce your T-cell count, and it is well-known that stress can damage your immune system. Meanwhile, positive emotions, such as the feelings of love, joy, enthusiasm, and so on, can have a beneficial effect on your health and well-being. I propose that it is well worth learning how to have better control over your reactions.

Controlling Your Reactions

The first step to controlling your reactions due to emotion is observation, which comes by increasing your self-awareness. To do this, you first need to pretend to observe yourself from a distance. Look at yourself in your mind's eye and create a picture of what you are feeling and how those feelings manifest. When you do this, you will begin to get a picture of who you really are. Your mind's eye will trace around your life and the effects that you've had on your body, internally and externally; and on your character. You may find that certain patterns repeat themselves and you can begin to understand what makes you react.

The second step is self-evaluation. With a better understanding of yourself, you can decide which reactions you want to change and which you want to keep. When you let go of a certain reaction, you may want to put a better one in its place. Understanding more about the other person can be put in place of reacting with anger. When you substitute understanding for anger, you are developing a new reaction. This new reaction will not only benefit you personally — it will also help the other person favor understanding, which will have a positive impact on your relationship. This kind of small, personal change can be the beginning of the development of a new skill; one that will enable you to have confidence in yourself and the process of change. You may experience slip-ups and regress into old patterns. However, as long as you keep practicing, you will keep growing.

Begin with a simple task, like saying "good morning" instead of frowning, and grow your practice from there. Remember that your health is at stake and you are the one in charge. If you consciously think you are in charge, you will consciously place yourself in charge. If you take this initiative to reflect and reclaim your reactions, you will be exercising your responsibility to yourself to be on the path of continual growth and enjoyment of the adventure of life. So remember: learn to control your negative emotions and enjoy your positive ones!

An Open Mind

Do you have an open mind? Or do you defend your thoughts, ideas and beliefs and live in a self-created prison? Very early in life, we are exposed to information from our environment that we must process and figure out. We are all exposed to stimuli — some different, some the same. But even twins have different environments. Young babies "absorb" emotions. For example, a mother who is anxious, angry and fearful around her child has a very different effect on her child than a loving and peaceful mother. Parental arguments affect children, too. As we grow up we learn things that we accept as true. Much of this information depends on our parents, relatives, teachers, religion, culture and geographic location. Children accept what their guardians say as true, until they see them argue. Then they begin questioning who we are meant to trust and even start to absorb some of the arguments. Things like believing that one religion is better than another, or that different skin colors have different importance are absorbed by children, especially if repeated often in a reactionary manner.

Some of us possess a false sense of "education." These people believe in what they have learned and and feel that it makes them who they are. These people are defensive of their beliefs and this defensive position "protects" them from having an open mind and allowing new information to enter and be evaluated. A closed, defensive mind makes us feel disinterested in pursuing a path of continuous learning. Ask yourself whether you have an open mind and a constant interest in learning. If you don't have an open mind, are you interested in learning how to get one? If you aren't even interested, that is really telling you something!

RESPONSIBILITY

"One day, in retrospect, the years of struggle will strike you as the most beautiful." — Sigmund Freud

The Responsibility Of All Practitioners

All doctors need to have a helpful heart. If you are a doctor, ask yourself: are you afraid of losing your patient to alternative therapies? If you work in the pharmaceutical industry, are you afraid of losing your job or income to alternative therapies? If you are a patient, can you afford to try all of the different healing modalities? Could you even afford to pay a holistic team to diagnose and treat you?

The idea of Holistic Integrative Treatment goes beyond personal health care and into the realm of collective health care. Taking care of our planet, our air, our soil and our water are all a part of our personal and collective health care journeys. Nearly everyone gets sick at some point in time, except perhaps a select few semi-isolated groups, like the Hunzakuts, who tend to die only of old age or accidents. As long as we continue to depend on our planetary environments, we need a soil that is free from chemicals and rich in nutrients, water that is clean from the source and not chlorinated or fluoridated, and air that is fresh and not full of impurities.

The current separations between prevention, diagnosis and treatment modalities do not create the most helpful paradigm for pursuing comprehensive health care. A new type of clinic known as the umbrella health clinic, sometimes referred to as a health spa, is a place where various health care services are offered in one building. There may be clinics for acupuncture, reiki, chiropractic, yoga, medical exams, etc. These are still separate services with little to no coordination or integration between shared patient diagnosis and treatment.

Taking a different approach, the Integrative Holistic Treatment clinic will have a team of practitioners from a variety of modalities. They will hold something called a "clinical conference" in which practitioners and patient would discuss a multidisciplinary approach to diagnosis, treatment, and future prevention. The team will also deliberate on the best tentative conclusions of the patient evaluation along with the patient's input. These multidimensional conclusions will be open to revision as new information is obtained.

Holistic team diagnosis is a prerequisite for holistic treatment. The holistic team can be conducted by a competent, mature, non-competitive leader, or a revolving leadership. A group process must develop intuitively in support of the group goal, which is the health of the patient. Individual health care practitioners will need to put aside their personal and professional egos; to eliminate competitiveness in the interest of the patient.

The patient must be prepared to hear conflicting information, which must necessarily be presented regardless of any resulting confusion. The patient can choose whether to be an active participant in the discussion, or they can passively answer questions and receive information at the direction of the group's leader. A complete lifestyle evaluation must be made, including a judgement of the patient's level of awareness of how their lifestyle influences disease. Appropriate goals and responsibility are determined together as a group so that successful efforts are made.

The complex process of Integrative Holistic Treatment can be made more comfortable in an atmosphere of understanding and love. The more that a holistic team works together, the more mature and intuitive the team will become. Understanding where and why disease is present is basic in the holistic diagnostic process. Alleviating symptoms is a secondary goal, but finding and treating the causes of disease is the ultimate goal of the integrative holistic team. The holistic health care team will aim to find the most helpful course of treatment can be recommended, and not be swayed by their corporate training in their recommendations. Helping the whole body, mind and spirit is the path to healing. Holistic detoxification and giving yourself what you really need, from nutrition to love, is the best way forward.

Holistic Integration Vs. Separation And Control

The concept of holistic healing goes beyond the body, mind, and spirit. It includes the environment and everything else in the universe. Everything affects everything. Holistic integration is infinite. There is no separation. The possibilities are so vast that a lifetime of study is not enough to fully comprehend or practice holistic living. To gain some awareness and consciousness of holistic practices, you need to begin with an open mind. Ask yourself: Do the stars affect my health? Does the water I drink affect my health? Does the food I eat affect my health? How do my emotions affect my health? How do my relationships, my job, the air I breathe, the soap I use, the city I live in, my cell phone, the doctors I listen to, my thoughts, the music I listen to affect my health? Everything is relative. When we understand this concept, we learn to accept our limitations and do the best we can. We can learn to give up the idea of separation and work to develop a more comprehensive view of the world in which we live. We are not separate from global politics, the banking systems, or the corporations around the world, so let us evaluate their effects on our health!

The need to survive and thrive teaches us to be practical. We tend to dismiss a more holistic picture in favor or listening to the most sensible sounding voice out of the group. In many cases, money speaks the loudest. When led by fear, we succumb to selling our freedom, our life, and our health to the loudest voices. We are trained to obey and compartmentalize and our "trainers" (the media, politicians, lobby groups, advertisers, educators, etc) use the separation of ideas to control our lives.

The healing arts have been controlled by money instead of compassion and love for long enough! The hearts of our healers have become cold and clinical. Practitioners need to open their hearts and minds, reduce their egos and learn to learn from one another. We hope that this book will act as an introduction to the practice of holistic living, helping practitioners and patients to bring together different understandings for a holistic view.

When you separate and isolate things, they naturally become easier to control. There are advantages to separation that help us study and understand individual parts in a system. However, taking things out of context can be misleading and it is important to maintain the awareness that the parts belong to a whole. Do not forget the holistic picture, even if you cannot apply it in the moment because it is this awareness that will keep you on the most helpful path for making decisions. Take some time to step back and think, rather than giving into your emotions in the moment. Don't look for the magical solution in which you can avoid effort and work in the moment. Grow into a mature sense of responsibility and step out of your learned helplessness. Do not be controlled by the controllers ("trainers") — learn to control yourself to bring you to your highest level of self development.

Personal Responsibility

To any logical adult, self-improvement is always possible. But many people are stuck in their limitations and afraid to admit that they are not perfect. Fear typically results in a fight or flight reaction, where you defend yourself or escape from the situation. Whichever reaction you have, you are still in need of development of your personal responsibility. But if you are motivated to grow and improve, your life will become healthier. Think logically and make the right choice.

A person with the symptoms of disease will go to see the doctor. The doctor asks the patient for the symptoms that brought them in. The patient tells the doctor their symptoms. These symptoms are warning signs for the patient and to doctor to pick up on, which point to the underlying causes of the symptoms. At this point, the doctor may treat the symptoms directly based on prior experiences with the same symptoms in the same context, or they may suggest various examinations or referrals for further study.

From an early stage in life, the responsibility for good health is placed upon the doctor rather than on both doctor and patient. The patient visits the doctors with the hopes of being cured of their symptoms. From early childhood, the patient has been given the message that the doctor has the cure for disease and will provide healing medicine. Whether this medicine comes in the form of pharmaceutical drugs, homeopathics, herbs, or energy healing, the patient is rarely told in these patient-practitioner encounters that the body has the capacity to cure itself, if given the helpful tools for health, while eliminating the harmful toxins. Instead, the patient has been conditioned to be a passive position regarding their health, where they will automatically defer to their health care practitioner. The patient concedes their care to the practitioner, rarely considering the doctor's potential or visible limitations. The practice of "alternative medicine" is growing, though, and both doctor and patient have become more open minded. But every practitioner is limited in the healing knowledge of modalities other than their own. For example, many allopathic doctors are aware of Traditional Chinese Medicine, but they may not have learned about tongue diagnosis or iridology diagnosis, or the relationship between our teeth and our organs.

There is a strong requirement for patient's to become active in their health care within the integrative holistic health care system. Patient passiveness is preferred in a system that relies upon treating as many patients as possible. Patients are financial assets in our current global health care systems. The patient must take an active role of responsibility for their health, understanding their symptoms, the causes of those symptoms, alternate diagnoses, and treatment of the presenting problems.

Ultimately, the body wants to heal itself. If we give it the right tools, it will return to its state of healthy functioning. All patients should be motivated to explore and study all of the available information about health, including anything on the forefront. The internet has an amazing amount of information that is easily available to the public, but there is still much information that can only be found in expensive medical journal subscriptions. Regardless of the availability of information, we have much room to evaluate our level of motivation; to rethink our daily routine; to be more efficient; and to prioritize our goals for better health. We cannot achieve optimal health without taking personal responsibility.

Free The Planet From The Slave Masters

Since the powers that be are receiving the full benefits and rewards of the systems that they have created for the status quo, they will not be motivated to change until the disadvantages of what they have created outweigh the rewards.

To heal the planet, it is up to us to first heal ourselves, and the air, water, soil, and more. Plants, animals, insects, fish and birds — our planet once thrived until we started to abuse it and it began dying prematurely as a result. It is high time that we look in the mirror and ask: why is it that we need to heal the planet and what has caused the planet to become what it is today? We cannot expect to "fix" anything until we change our thinking; until we understand the problem, and until we are ready with active solutions. Our thoughts and our emotions contribute to our actions. If our fears, insecurities, self-doubts, and greed continue to dominate our love, the path of self-destruction continues to unfold before us. Our world leaders (subject to the powers that be) will face the real issues within themselves, too. They will seek to change their motivations through expanding their consciousness to receive more new information every day. Each of us must do the same — let go of hopelessness, impotence, and resignation. We must take appropriate action, such as buying only unprocessed foods and supporting local, organic farmers. It is crucial that we educate children to be wary of propaganda in the media by teaching them the truth about living a healthy lifestyle.

Our focus must be held on restoring ourselves so that we can let nature restore itself, too. Nature knows what must be done to regenerate back to a healthful state. Our bodies also know what to do when we give them the right nutrients to meet our needs. Holistic healers are growing in consciousness and in numbers, and we will continue to do so. Start improving yourself today by asking what you want for your future and what you are willing to do today to achieve it. Those who continuously seek more are never fulfilled with the state of their own selves. Perhaps they are enamored with the power and control they have already amounted. They experience difficulty looking inside themselves because there is no true desire, capability or motivation outside of obtaining more. Some wake up when they are close to death and some never do because they are counting their money until the last day and still seeking control. Is it actually less that we need? Perhaps that's not the best way to phrase it, either. There are some things that we are certain must be eliminated and we must each develop our own will to change our choices. It is our time to simplify our wants in order to harmonize more easily and readily with our true bodily and planetary needs.

There Are No Gurus

Yes, you have all the power. It all lies within you. All you have to do is to learn how to use it. For many years, gurus have sold themselves under various names, finding buyers who are seeking to save or better themselves.

In the last 25 years, these master marketers have made billions of dollars thanks to good marketing and a public seeking short cuts or magical solutions. They are not aware of their inner ability to heal. Take a look around on the internet and you will find many sites selling you something in every imaginable arena of your life. Have you spent any money on any of them lately?

Internet Money Gurus want to make money from selling you their products. Many of them utilize information from psychology, neurology, Chinese medicine, psychoanalysis, etc. They are very clever in selling techniques and offer certification such as a certified dream coach, in their programs. Their offerings are aimed to help you help yourself and others. One of the bottom lines is making money for you and them. All that is ok. They offer you a win/win situation. Everything is made to look easy and simple and they offer special bargains. They claim their techniques will change your life quickly.

I offer a word of caution: do not chase the carrot and pay for the chase. Real growth is usually a process rather than a single magical jump. People do not usually unlearn their life history and make lifestyle changes that last without doing the the step by step work that is necessary. Your body is programmed to heal itself and you can learn to assist it with the right information and the right nutrition for energetically healing itself. This information includes the ideas of physical karma, mental karma, emotional and spiritual dimensions. Understanding energy systems in your body and how to give them what they need promotes your capacity to heal, love and enjoy yourself. When you realize this you will realize we are all equal in our capacity to self-heal and self-govern. We heal ourselves—others can only help us to find the way. Only we can do the healing within ourselves so we must make the responsible choices. Not even the person in the white coat can help you, especially if their prime motivator is what is making you worse as your doctor continues to profit from your illness until the day you die.

When you buy into the system you are trained to buy into, you give up your responsibility to educate yourself. You pass this laziness onto future generations of brainwashed children who will continue to seek healing from outside of themselves. There is no need to continue to live with pain or low energy. Learn how to use our own power to create optimal energy in your life. When you develop the right attitude, beliefs, thinking free from emotional blocks, detoxification, good nutrition, good sleeping habits, exercise and breathing, you will be better prepared to develop and become conscious of the spirit that you already are. You don't need to continue to live your everyday life controlled by the habits, emotions, feelings, addictions and other past wounds to your being. You can free yourself and live the life that you want to live.

If You Don't, Who Will?

To heal the planet we must first heal ourselves, our minds, bodies, emotions and spirit. We must look in the mirror and deep inside ourselves and find the causes of our self destructive thinking. We can't "fix" anything until we change our thinking. Our thinking influences our emotions both of which contribute to our actions. If fear, insecurities, self doubts and greed continue to dominate our love, spirit and hope, the path of self destruction will continue to increase its hold on you. When irrational power and money control the minds of the powers that be because they get the benefits and rewards of the status quo, they are not motivated to change. We must change and end our hopelessness, impotence, passivity, futility and resignation.

When we change our motivations and consciousness nature will restore itself. Nature knows what to do just as our bodies know what to do given the right nutrients. Most technological discoveries have lead to increased pollution, new diseases such as childhood cancer and diabetes, atomic waste disposal problems, harmful drugs, unnatural and processed foods. When we disturb and destroy nature we destroy ourselves. We are a part of nature and not separate from it. We continue to learn the power of nature's forces when we abuse it. We must live in harmony with nature, each other and within ourselves. We must focus on our common goals not our differences. Our lives must be directed towards our spiritual growth, with love, peace, faith, brotherhood and hope at the forefront. We are growing in consciousness and numbers and will continue to do so if you start improving yourself today. If you don't, who will?

Speak Up, World!

You have the courage inside you to change and it will grow in you when you start to use it. You must use it to change yourself, your family, community, nation and the world. You are challenged by internal fear, cast upon you by the false, external powers that threaten you. These powers are self serving and intimidate those that get in their way or do away with them.

What happened to *your* voice? What happened to *your* thoughts? The right to express your thoughts has been guaranteed to you, yet you hold back your words. Many of you are waiting for safety before you speak up; however, if you don't speak up, you will not find safety. Your single voice, multiplied by many others, can create the world you want and need to live, and a life of truth, wisdom and compassion.

Speak up and change yourself. Make good choices or continue to watch your life go by while you feel helpless and controlled by false powers. Each person who speaks up encourages another to do the same is spreading power. Speaking up gives you real power, which grows in you, the community, the nation and the world. It starts with each of us, eventually spreading to most of us, and finally to all.

Living in fear promotes thought. Thought can stimulate the challenge of courage. Having courage then presents you with a choice to make: stay where you are; or risk going forward and growing your inner power. Delay facing this challenge and you will weaken yourself. Face this challenge and you will feel the joy of growth. Only you can make this correct choice. Summon your courage, strength, determination and make the commitment to make a responsible choice for yourself and humanity!

Speak up, world!

If You Don't Wake Up Now, You Will Die Prematurely

Millions of people die prematurely of degenerative diseases, heart attacks, strokes and cancer. The statistics are there to prove it; however, little attention is paid to them because most people have become rigid in their thoughts and attitudes. Even if they are willing to listen to helpful information, they soon disregard it and go on their usual way. When people ingest toxins and other harmful substances, they will surely suffer the consequences of doing so. And even though they know this, they continue to harm themselves. What is it about their thinking and psychological makeup that allows them to be addicted to self-destructive behavior? Do they love their food and other addictions more than their own lives? Is the denial mechanism so strong that they cannot act rationally?

After many years of being conditioned by repeating negative habits, it is not easy to make changes. Most people have great difficulty when they try to change their eating habits because they enjoy certain tastes. For example, trying to eat food without salt is a change that people find hard to do. Many people do not know what unsalted food tastes like. They have grown up with salt and sugar and find food to be tasteless without their addition. So what is the remedy for these patterns of self-destruction? When the advertising media bombards the world with its products, how can people learn to make healthier choices?

Medical technology is more advanced than it ever has been. Pharmaceutical products have reached an all time high. Biotechnology has made incredible advances in cloning, transplants and artificial body parts. Many billions of dollars are spent annually on research to cure cancer. The vitamin industry has grown enormously. Despite all this, as well as other scientific advances, cancer is on the rise and childhood cancer and diabetes now exist. Cardiovascular diseases are still the number one killers.

Think about saving your own life and the lives of your family by questioning the official narratives. Why wait to receive a triple bypass, radiation, chemotherapy or surgery? Wake up now and learn how to live a healthier lifestyle today

Dr. Walter J. Urban with Alexandra Luty

Grassroots Of The World

True strength and power lies in the spirit of the people of the world as a whole. It does not lie in the individual governments and politicians, nor in any world authorities like the World Bank, IMF, United Nations, or the Bank of International Settlements. And it does it lie in any nation's Gross Domestic Product, stock markets, advanced technologies, Federal Reserve, oil reserves, uranium deposits, or anything else of value created by an individual or group of humans.

The spirit of the people and the natural forces of the universe are the true foundations of the energy that guides us. When these two work in harmony, as part of each other, we create a world of love, wisdom, clarity, peace, compassion, and responsible choice. When the spirit and the consciousness of the people become suppressed and lost in the chaos of materialism, greed and destruction, we become resigned to helplessness and hopelessness. When we wake up to our inner selves and realize our intrinsic self-worth, we respect ourselves and each other. We bond together in freedom and respect our differences instead of trying to force our ways onto others.

When we let go of overconsumption, we will realize that there is enough for everyone. When we let go of our fears, insecurities and feelings of powerlessness, we will feel strength, love, and inner-peace. This will lead us to a more spiritual path; one which has a unifying effect. Our grassroots spiritual unity will be an effective voice that governments, politicians, and other so-called world leaders will follow because we will be the awakened, conscious majority. We, the people of the world; the grassroots, will restore integrity to the chaotic destruction that must stop before it is too late. Awaken yourself and those in your personal world to our shared need of promoting our personal integrity and power so we may all live the lives that we want, rather than the life forced upon us.

INSURANCE, CANCER AND DRUGS

There are three institutions that are so entrenched in the medical community that it is difficult to imagine a future without them. They are insurance, cancer, and pharmaceutical drugs. Each are killers in their own right, stifling any evolutions made in health care with their absolute might.

The multi-billion dollar health insurance industry is essentially a gatekeeper for modern health care. A vast population of people cannot afford to pay for private treatment and are therefore restricted access to that which—in theory, is meant to protect their lives. Cancer, in all of its forms, is the biggest killer on our planet. And the pharmaceutical industry has become so big that it controls much of the innovation in health care.

The Cancer Lie

Have you ever wondered why the numerous medical associations dedicated to cancer research have not found a cure for cancer in the last fifty years of study? In that time, there have been hundreds of new drugs and medical equipment developed in the fight against cancer and yet the American Cancer Society predicts that one out of every two men and one out of three women will get cancer in their lifetimes. Despite these numbers, the two major treatments of cancer are still radiation and chemotherapy — both of which cause damage to healthy body parts.

The cancer "industry" is a lucrative business. It is a suspicious coincidence that around fifteen doctors from the United States who claimed to have found a cure for cancer have been found dead (at last count, the estimated number of recent mysterious deaths of holistic practitioners is around

90). If true, this is a tragedy on a grand scale that vested interests in the medical industry are actively working to stop the release of a cure for any disease, let alone one that is a multi-billion dollar industry. However, this pattern is being broken as allopathic doctors are helping to treat cancer with detoxification and good nutrition.

In his book, The Politics of Cancer (1978), Samuel S. Epstein, M.D., backed by meticulous documentation, charges that the cancer establishment remains myopically fixated on damage control—diagnosis and treatment, and basic genetic research with not always benign indifference to cancer prevention research and failure of outreach to Congress, regulatory agencies, and the public with scientific information on unwitting exposures to a wide range of avoidable causes of cancer.

Cancer is currently thought to be caused by a combination of factors that include eating foods with chemicals, lacking the right nutrients in the diet, possessing negative emotions and thoughts, breathing toxic air, absorbing toxic chemicals through the skin, absorbing radiation, and other unnatural processes. Treating cancer by the now traditional methods of radiation and chemotherapy have been proven exponentially harmful. Implementing them alone or as a first resort makes them dangerous treatments.

The cutting edge treatments of cancer, like the Dr. Gerson method, are currently being revisited thanks to medical researchers like Ty Bollinger, who wrote The Truth About Cancer (2016). In his work, Bollinger re-opens the subject on new cures for cancer that bypass the need for more harmful chemicals and radiation. I was on the Board of Directors at the Gerson Institute in San Diego, California many years ago. They are a non-profit organization dedicated to providing education and training in the Gerson Therapy, an alternative, non-toxic treatment for cancer and other chronic degenerative diseases. The institute was forced to move to Mexico in 2014 because Dr. Gerson's program was able to cure cancer, including cases of pancreatic cancer going into remission.

The American Cancer Society's approved diet contains aspartame (an artificial sweetener), fluoride, high sugar foods, canned foods, sliced bread, processed foods, and irradiated foods. They also promote cheese and other dairy products as good sources of calcium and eating fruit with every meal[26]. They even say that it is safe to consume limited amount of fried foods. This information is incorrect and the consumption of these foods contributes to the production of cancer cells. The American Cancer Society helps build the cancer industry with these outrageous claims.

Harry Edwards, former president of the British National Federation of Spiritual Healers, states in his book, The Healing Intelligence (1965), that the intelligence of a cell "has been likened to that of the mind" (page 77). When a person becomes frustrated, possibly due to fear, grief, shock, or disappointment, that person's mental processes will suffer, creating the conditions for disease. Continual frustration leads to cell dysfunction. Edwards concludes that cancer can be caused psychosomatically. Very rarely, though, does an allopathic doctor actually investigate the possibility of mental and emotional factors contributing to illnesses like cancer. Inner self-frustrations may be hidden ones and bottled up feelings do not release the tensions they cause on their own. Each cell needs the right nutrition and elimination of its wastes. When the cell is stressed by various frustrations and cannot function properly, its functions are impeded and it becomes a sick cell. Repeated stress hammers away at it, making it more dysfunctional. Eventually, the neighboring cells are affected and sick cells continue to grow and spread, which may cause a tumor. This important cause of cancer is almost never properly investigated by qualified health care practitioners, yet it is not a new discovery.

Cancer is a very lucrative "business" for those who earn money from it. I would personally love to receive the opportunity to work with cancer patients as a psychoanalyst and clinical psychologist. It is well-known to myself and many others that stress can cause bodily changes. Those of us who consider ourselves to be healing facilitators must recognize that only the body heals itself. Suppressing or repressing emotions shifts them to the unconscious mind and buried emotions will affect a body by attacking its cells.

---

[26] https://www.cancer.org/healthy/eat-healthy-get-active/eat-healthy.html

The body's intelligence can clean a wound and form a blood clot to close a wound. It can also fix the cells affected by cancer with proper directions from itself. Any doctor, including those from the allopathic modalities; who are treating a cancer patient will acknowledge that, in spite of whatever treatment the patient receives, the patient's body must also do its share of the healing work to get results. The patient's outlook, attitude, and thoughts must be of hope, combined with expectancy, that their spiritual, mental and bodily intelligences will heal the problem. The patient cannot concede to a state of hopelessness, despair and fear *and* expect healing. Healing will advance when this is recognized and taught in professional training programs for the integration of modalities. We must remember the harmony and balance that is needed between body, mind, emotions and spirit.

In 2017, there were approximately 1,688,780 new cancer cases diagnosed and 600,920 cancer deaths in the US alone. Let us help this epidemic come to an end.

The Role Of Insurance And Pharmaceutical Companies

Communication and camaraderie are needed — today as much as always — between the different health care professions and the insurance companies. Insurers stand to benefit from the addition of more modalities into their system. Alternative modalities employ many doctors who have patients dependent on them.

Insurance companies are hugely profitable and involved in every industry in the world. Every corporation buys insurance. They provide many benefits like emergency care and good quality examinations. However, they also possess great wealth and exert power over the rules and regulations of their doctors. And currently, the main treatment tools that insurance companies support are drugs and surgery. It is unfortunate that insurance doctors are trapped by this type of insurance structure. These doctors only have a limited amount of time to consult with a patient because the current model focuses on quick turn around for more prescriptions to be written.

The insurance corporations are so powerful that they appear to have control over regulatory boards. The pharmaceutical corporations that supply the insurance providers are giant monopolies, too, that have control over much of the allopathic education system. These doctors are taught to be drug-oriented when prescribing symptom relief. As a result, a large majority of patients have become drug-dependent due to the undesirable side effects of prescription drugs. Drugs have the ability to prolong disease while the business of treatment remains strong and suffering continues.

Insurance companies have two strikes against them: they are typically public companies, subject to shareholders; and they have many rules to follow in diagnosing and treating their patients. They need to show profits to their shareholders in order to survive within a free market economy. Their CEOs and other officers have very high salaries and to keep them that way the doctors must "produce," and the company must show profits. Expenses must be minimized, consultations become time-limited and referrals to specialists and exams are economically- and time-constrained.

A personal example of this was when a private care doctor gave differing advice to my primary care doctor, who refused to acknowledge the suggestions. My primary care doctor opted to use the insurance-sanctioned protocols, rather than proceeding with the tests suggested by the private practitioner. This meant that I had to endure a long wait for test results that could have helped me sooner. These types of patient-doctor proceedings are typical, although they are not good practice when it comes to patient care. It is a system that is money first, patient second. Saving and delaying visits to specialists reduces a primary care doctor's insurance expenses.

Examples of health care stocks with dividends are Abbott Laboratories, which paid 2.8% and had a 47% return, as compared to the S&P 500 in 2017, which had a lower return. Merck & Co pay 3% dividends, and Johnson&Johnson pay 2.8%. Public companies will do anything to make money for stockholders. And when our health care industry is populated by public companies looking to fulfill their duties to their shareholders, this means that things like unnecessary surgeries and treatments, or long wait times and service cuts become the norm.

The first realistic step to change would be to demand that insurance industries accept different modalities into their insurance system. Patient money will be saved by quicker and more efficient treatments, less surgeries, as well as good disease prevention programs. And by working within an integrative holistic health care system, we can guarantee more complete healing for all patients. The current system of "health care" needs to be improved to become patient care oriented and not money care focused.

So what happens to the good doctor who is overloaded with patients and limited for time? What happens to his heart and empathy when he is "trapped" by debt and other financial situations? The doctor may have a good heart but stockholders want a dividend and to see the stock price rise. Is there any motivation left for looking after the needs of the patient? The intention behind the treatment can affect the doctor, the patient and their relationship. A doctor with the intention of "processing" diagnoses and treatments in '15 insurance minutes' cannot have the same healing effect as one who really cares and does not set restrictive time limits, or any other limits. It is inherently obvious which type of service the majority of patients would prefer.

Direct primary care is a small but fast-growing movement of allopathic doctors who don't accept insurance and instead charges a monthly membership fee. At a time when many are feeling pressure from high health care costs, direct primary-care models can be a cheaper alternative that offers quick access to doctors and sometimes wholesale prices on medications or lab tests. This model is getting a lot of interest from young doctors, residents, and medical students, who see it as an alternative to the traditional fee-for-service health care model. But there are still challenges that face the movement—from insurers pushing back on the model to issues related to the movement's fast growth.

Drugs, Drugs, Drugs

For many years, drug companies have held major influence over allopathic medical education. Doctors are trained in the use of drugs. These drugs are prescribed for most patients after a consultation. These drugs are mainly used to relieve symptoms while the intensive study of the cause of the symptoms is neglected. Almost all allopathic drugs weaken the system and have side effects that may likely cause other symptoms — now or in the future. One well known example of this is that antibiotics destroy the good microbes as well as the bad, leaving room for viruses to mutate. Statin drugs are another example that are prescribed to fight cardiovascular disease. Among other side effects, the two major negative effects associated with statin drugs are: rhabdomyolysis, a serious condition in which cells of muscles become damaged; and liver damage, which can occur when statins cause an increase in liver enzymes to aid in digestion. These types of drugs prescribed when there are simpler lifestyle recommendations that can be made to fight things like cardiovascular disease.

Leading clinical nutritionist, Dr. Patrick Quillin, views the planet earth as our greatest pharmacy and says that we are ignoring many of its treatments. In the United States, around $280 billion is spent a year on prescription drugs.[27] According to the Journal of the American Medical Association, there are 140,000 Americans who die each year from the on-label use of prescription drugs, following their doctor's orders. This puts prescription drugs somewhere around the third leading cause of death in America from using drugs that are rarely helpful and often toxic!

Peter C. Gotzsche, MD is the cofounder of The Cochrane Collaboration — a global independent network of researchers, professionals, patients formed to organize medical research findings. They aim to facilitate evidence-based choices about health interventions. Dr. Gotzsche says that two years ago, he found out that prescription drugs are the third leading cause of death after heart disease and cancer. "Our drugs kill about 200,000 people in America every year and half of these people die while they do what their doctors told them. So they die because of the side-effects. The other half die because of the errors and it's often the doctors that make the errors because any drug may come with 20, 30, or 40 warnings, counter indications, precautions and so on. And no doctor knows about all of

---

[27] Brill, Stephen. *Bitter Pill: Why Medical Bills Are Killing Us.* Time Magazine. 2013.

this, so they give patients drugs that they should not have given them that interact dangerously with other drugs and food allergies."[28]

There are some exceptions where drugs are necessary for emergency treatment but these instances are fewer than we are led to believe by allopathic medicine as supported by the pharmaceutical and insurance industries. It is clearly known that the amount of new drugs prescribed increases each year, and new labels are given to long-known conditions like restless leg syndrome, which is something that is now treated with drugs. What was once called a nervous child, and later a hyperactive child, is now a sufferer of Attention Deficit and Hyperactivity Disorder, and new drugs are prescribed with every shift in diagnosis. New syndromes equal increased business developments for drug companies. And a lack of information and education in patients and practitioners perpetuates the use of drugs.

[28] https://www.youtube.com/watch?v=dozpAshvtsA

SPIRITUALITY

"We cannot change anything unless we accept it." —Carl Jung

Wherever it is that you want to go, it's good to get there in small steps. Changing your brain chemistry with a shock treatment can elicit positive changes in your life, but it is a reactive state rather than a reflective state, which means that you may miss the important lessons that come with making mindful changes. And to be more spiritual, we need to get to where we want to go in stages, so that the mind and body are able to understand, accept, and assist in the changes that our spirit's seek.

A central belief in shamanism is that whenever you learn to face the fact that you are going to die, that is when you develop a sense of freedom. Learn to face this greatest of fears now and eliminate it. This is the first step to developing and growing your spirituality because the fear of death is our greatest obstacle to being free. Some shamans believe that we also have two other fears: that of insecurity; and of old age, disease and suffering.

Spirituality can mean different things to different people. Below are a few questions to help you consider what spirituality might mean to you, since it is so difficult to define in a general sense. Try to answer some of these questions before reading the next paragraph:

Are you aware of being spiritual?
Do you take time to think about or look at your spirituality?
Does spirituality exist for you?
Does it exist, even if you don't believe in it?
Where does it exist?
Is it real, or is it only a belief, or even a state of mind?
What is spirituality?
Do you believe in spirit's ability to help conquer your worries and fears of lack of support, old age, disease and death?
Is spirit energy, even though it is immaterial?
If you are strong willed, do you need to be spiritual?
Is spirituality founded in love and compassion?
Are you spiritual, even if you don't believe in it?
Do you need to think about it to be spiritual, or is it there all the time?
Do humans create the concept of spirituality?
Are animals birds, fish and plants spiritual?

Spirit is immaterial. It has been called a vital principle in humans and animals. The word 'spirit' is derived from the latin word *spiritus* referring to soul, courage, vigor and breath. It is something that transcends the boundaries of the body and the mind.

Spirituality has traditionally been connected with religion and with the image of God, or the idea of divine entities. The notion of spirituality recently shifted to being perceived as a sacred dimension thanks to modern day physics. It can be conceived of as a supernatural force that is not observable but present, nonetheless. For instance, neuroscientists have found that spiritual experiences can have powerful effects on a person's neurotransmitters. Modern spirituality focuses on value and the meaning of life. It is an inward path to the essence of our being. Modern spiritual practices may include deprivation aimed at purifying the body, and minimizing and purifying the ego's self-centeredness in favor of unity and connection to the divine All.

The purpose here is not to make a study of spirituality, but rather to understand how it relates to and affects health and health care. Since each of us have our own definition and practice of spirituality, let us establish a baseline that we can all follow along to:

Can someone who eats meat be spiritual, even if the animal is killed by someone else?

Is spirituality learned, or is everyone spiritual, whether they are aware of it or not?

Are there different levels of spirituality to be obtained?

Is someone who hurts others spiritual?

How does spirit relate to politicians, corporations, law makers, bankers, media people, etc.?

Is spirituality a necessary part of good health care; to help the person's belief about healing?

Spirituality is a necessary part of good health care because it helps people believe that there is a purpose to healing and living. When we believe that we are all connected by spirit, we find value in life that extends beyond our individual ego. Holistic integration can be established as a core value and the foundation of attaining good health because we recognize that we are all different in our reactions, but in our reflections we can find commonality. We can achieve the best health when we cleanse ourselves of negative thoughts, feelings, and behaviors, which separate us from each other. Answering the above questions will help us establish our global baseline for the purpose and value of life, and lead us towards harmony.

We Are Not Separate

When we inhale and exhale, we connect to the air that everyone is breathing. When we eat, we connect to the planet from which we all feed. It is your ego that separates you from others in your mind. It is really that simple, and yet our human history trains us to have different beliefs. We are trained, brain washed, conditioned to feel removed from the natural world in our minds, and our shared processes are made to feel automatic or reactive, rather than reflective. The purpose of this type of conditioning is to gain and maintain control of power and money.

We are slowly killing ourselves with radiation, GMOs, pollution, drugs, the wrong fatty foods, and more. What some might call "progress" may not be progress for other or the planet. When we kill weeds with Roundup, we poison our soil and food.[29] Successful societies throughout history, like the Incas, grew a lot of food and did not poison the planet or themselves while doing so.

What may have begun as spirituality in humans was turned into religion for profit and for power. Many of the religions throughout time divided people in order to conquer them. In much the same way, the exchange of goods in a marketplace eventually evolved into the Federal Reserve banking system, which has let the US into a $21.6 trillion debt today.[30] From simplicity to a gradual self-destruction, we went from human hands and the plow to nuclear weapons. Here we are, struggling and struggling, each day faster and faster, more and more.

Religions may have different names for their gods but they are all synonyms for energy. Religions place their ideas of power in the hands of gods which are seen as an external force, meaning that for most religions, power is thought to be outside of the self. Spirituality and energy may be one and the same. Scientists have agreed that everything is composed of energy, which cannot be created or destroyed. Buddhism sees the power inside

---

[29] https://www.the-scientist.com/news-opinion/how-toxic-is-the-worlds-most-popular-herbicide-roundup-30308

[30] http://www.usdebtclock.org/

yourself, which is a very different belief to most religions, and yet in alignment with the most progressive ideas in modern science.

Separation, on the other hand, leads to negative thoughts and actions that cause destruction. But faith and hope can be had in both internal and external forces; in God and in yourself. What is important is that we learn how to manage our egos and feel that if all is one, then the idea of "god" cannot exist without it idea of "I" and vice versa, yet neither has power over the other. And so it doesn't matter what you believe in, whether it's in God or in yourself; what counts is that you believe at all. Many of us are invested in our beliefs because we have been taught that is who we are, so it is going to take an open mind to start to think about the idea of "power" over our lives, and about not separating ourselves from others or from our place on the planet. We are interdependent, and the powers that be, or the controllers of our planet's resources like the banks, corporations and media, will one day sees that they are no longer able to control us, despite their efforts. By increasing our consciousness, awareness, and consideration of our place in the whole, we take back our power to create. We are not separate and our interconnectedness is the foundation for the integrative holistic view.

Dissolving The Unuseful Parts Of The Ego

What does dissolving the unuseful part of your ego mean? A simple understanding of ego is that it is the idea you have of who you are. Ego makes use of your senses and what you think, feel and do. This is a simplified definition, so if you need a more detailed understanding, please check the nearest wiktionary. Instead, we would like to focus on what it means to dissolve the parts of the ego that don't serve your health.

The unuseful parts of your ego can be explained as those times when you think you are better than someone else; or when you possess more information about something than someone else and you see them as inferior; or when you do something to show off how smart you are. Suspend any idea of who you experience as yourself under normal circumstances. Maybe this sounds unusual or crazy, but people do this all of the time, like those who use mind-altering substances to think, feel and act differently to their "normal self."

It is commonly accepted that all matter is energy. Quantum physics can help us understand that we, and everything else, are made of particles of energy that have come together in our unique form. These particles create us and all that we think, feel, and do. Energy is often defined as the capacity to do work, so these particles of energy that fill our being are the basic elements of our total being. They manifest in different forms, ranging from humans to rocks, plants, cars, animals, tables, thoughts, lungs, livers, hearts, spirits, and anything else you can think of. Everything has a common denominator of this basic energy therefore it is logical that this basic energy applies to everything and all of us. There is a basic connection between everything. If we can accept this, we will realize that we all have the force of one energy in common. In this connection, we realize that there are no real differences between us when we all come from the same energy. Difference implies separation, and we are only different in our egos.

It has been observed throughout history that our differences lead to conflicts that lead to wars and other destructive actions. When we learn to temporarily suspend the idea of our differences, the world could function more constructively. We would not waste energy on reacting to our differences and we could channel our energy to solving collective problems, like our health and the health of our planet. When we learn how to consciously dissolve the unuseful parts of our egos, we will experience this basic energy that we are all composed of and consciously control outcomes by tracing their paths through our shared energy.

Learning how to exercise conscious control is something that can be achieved through meditation, affirmation, and creation. Exercising conscious control is temporarily dissolving the negative parts of the ego and then regaining control over the ego. When this is directly experienced it is much different than reading or talking about it because we learn that there is no separation and all is one and the same. Even when we go back into thinking, feeling and acting in our ego, we will forever remember the experience of oneness. It is a door that cannot (and should not) be closed once it is open.

When there finally is no separation, we will begin to see ourselves and the planet as one type of energy, manifested in different forms. We will dissolve the barriers caused by the differences in power and control between everyone and everything. We will recognize that we can all exercise the same power and control. When we see ourselves and the planet as a single family unit, we will become actively harmonious, consciously working and living for our mutual goals.

To achieve this state of experienced awareness requires the desire and motivation to learn how to take power away from the egoic forces of control that have been in operation throughout history. For those of us who lack the awareness of these forces, they are entrenched in their egos and are committed to separation and the destruction that it causes. Motivate yourself to understand more about dissolving your ego for your own benefit, for your family's, and for all of humankind and our shared planet.

Ego isn't all negative. We also need our egos to function. The aforementioned paragraphs are theoretical and are not practical. Life does not exist in theory alone but rather alongside an active ego. The point being made is that we need to be aware of our egos and to choose to function with positive thoughts, feelings and emotions.

Better Education

Life is precious. Living things on the planet are not separate from the planet. Air, water, and soil are not separate from the planet. They are not separate from the world's governments, politics, media, corporations, and banks, either. Everything works together because we live in a controlled system that can be defined as energy. To achieve optimum health, helpful information is needed — the type that will benefit all of humanity. Instead, mind-controlling misinformation is offered to us by the powers that be, who want to turn the world into a slave state, run by a single, insane, suicidal, psychopathic, and murderous government.

Our consciousness of the instruments of separation and control has been growing rapidly since the advent of the Internet. As more people wake up and see reality more clearly, they can escape the controlled patterns of thoughts, feelings and actions. We can increase our awareness of the food we eat, the air we breathe, the water we drink, the drugs we take, the radiation we absorb, and so on. We can free ourselves from the unconscious slavery that we live in by becoming conscious of it. We can reevaluate our beliefs, taking them out of the controlled matrix; reevaluate the education that we received from authorities, like parents, our teachers, doctors, or the media. We can reevaluate everything by taking responsibility for learning of our own volition and using an open mind to eliminate the misinformation, lies, propaganda, that we have been limited by. We can replace the old systems of control — the matrices that we operate within — with new, fresh information that is filled with more truth. We can make the right choices for our health, the health of our children, and that of our planet. We can escape the Grand Matrix, designed by the old controllers, who use unconscious subliminal programming to train our egos and take power away from our choices.

The Grand Matrix teaches us to buy toothpaste that is filled with the neurotoxin, fluoride. It teaches us to buy new smartphones and bigger television screens every year. The educational system can be revised to teach children about their health and that of the planet. We can teach children that consuming food with over 10,000 additives is not healthy; or that consuming animals injected with hormones and antibiotics is not healthy; or that taking pharmaceutical drugs prescribed by allopathic doctors is not the solution. This education can start at an early age and needs to teach critical, creative thinking, imagination and responsibility. The education of allopathic doctors needs to maintain what Hippocrates taught: to do no harm. This tenet is in the oath of western, allopathic practitioners, which means that they need to evaluate the effects of chemotherapy and radiation on cancer patients and study the value that whole foods, sleep and exercise have on healing.

Let Go

Let go of who you think and believe you are. With eyes closed, concentrate on the idea that you are made of vibrating specks of live energy, dancing around in your mind's eye. Can you imagine yourself as these pulsating dynamic specks of light talked about in quantum physics? If you can believe that the universe is made up of particles or units of energy and that everything boils down to moving energy, then you may want to try the following imagination exercise:

Speak with the tongue of the feeling heart and spirit — not only with the tongue of words.

Radiate energy from your heart — not only with the logic of the limited mind, trained by the slave masters, who teach conformity and obedience in their product messages.

Close your eyes and let your inner rivers of energy and spirit carry you — without fear of the unknown. Float down the river with patience and love — don't swim.

Feed on the formless universal energy — don't try to understand what has yet to be labeled. Trust in the unknown and let it carry you, with its ebb and flow, to the edge of your consciousness. Let the current peacefully take you beyond your former limits.

Do not be intimidated by worldly affairs — they are in their own evolution and lead to their own natural consequences. Let the laws of nature prevail over human illusions.

Enter into the realm of heart-light-feeling-spirit by not trying to enter it — only then can it come. The feeling heart of love and compassion are inseparable. Energy and spirit moves everything and will bring you peace and healing.

CONCLUSION

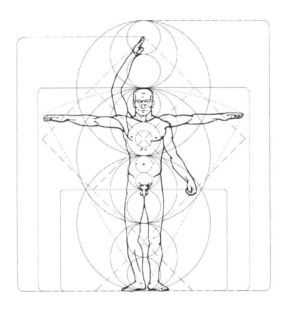

"One can have no smaller or greater mastery than mastery of oneself." — Leonardo da Vinci

The Future

With all of the themes of this book in mind, we hope that you can see the need for Integrative Holistic Team Diagnosis. Understanding all of these themes takes time and patience from the doctor who is rushed by financial pressures, and from the patient who is rushed to get back to their "normal life."

The 'Integrative Holistic Team' offers many advantages over a single practitioner. In the work of Irving Jamus, <u>Victims of GroupThink</u> (1972), the author describes the psychology of members of a group. For instance, allopathic medicine practitioners tend to have the idea of being invulnerable in their collective rationalization. They often believe that they alone are right and that outsiders with ideas different to their own are not knowledgeable. The person with a closed mind continues to defend their position.

In a holistic team we must never lose sight of the need to help. The integrative holistic team can be of great value to patients who will recover faster because doctors give better help and both doctor and patient have improved the openness of their minds. Doctors will live longer, utilizing a more integrative holistic therapy model. They are, after all, their own future patients.

The Vision

The shaman visualizes what forces do not exist in the material world. He is not only a dreamer but also a thinker, connected to a special consciousness and unconsciousness.

Integrative holistic theory goes beyond health care. health care is an aspect of holistic living, as well as the holistic planet and the holistic universe. We are not separate from the sun, air, water and soil. The content of this book separates 'health care' from the universe in an attempt to help people achieve better health. But when we separate things, we also lose some of the information that is found in the connection between. Everything is more than the sum of its parts.

Better lives can be lived with the knowledge we humans have already uncovered in modern medicine. What is available now may be limited in and of itself; however, new frontiers and new information are constantly being discovered, though they were in existence all of the time. The first step in integrative holistic therapy is consciousness. As humanity develops more consciousness—of ourselves and of the external world, and as we develop greater heart consciousness, we have the hope and belief that we can improve our total health. I choose the path of action. I don't stop at thoughts. Step by step, I proceed. I, too, am more than a dreamer. When I wrote the book <u>Integrative Therapy Foundation For Holistic and Self-Healing</u> (1978), I saw how the therapies I knew at the time needed to work together and that separation created limitations.

Thought and intention are the mother of action in most cases. Action-taking uses forethought, which helps us visualize what has a good chance of becoming reality in a step-by-step manner. It is best not to spend too much energy visualizing what is not likely to happen in the near future. Don't lose energy on illusions. Instead, spend more energy on action in support of the visualization. Visualization may strengthen the action, however don't visualize the impossible happening now.

There have been times when those who introduce and teach visualization have packaged and sold what may be considered *false hopes*. Try visualizing getting a new car in the next month and tell me what happens. Visualize being in perfect health in the future and choose to make realistic goals on which you can take immediate action in support of this visualization.

Now, my hope is that the time has come for the integration of therapies, as shown by what is already taking place in summits, therapy centers, and general dialogue. People are looking for change to the current health care standards and wanting to experience real healing of the cause of their disease. Progress has been happening at its own pace due to the many forces of selfish personal interest that limit a healthy human progress. But with increased consciousness, the old forces are being torn down. New frontiers in nutrition, stem cell therapy, bioelectronics, and more are in progress. As this evolution takes place, humanity gains more openness and sincerity from the hearts and minds of the leaders in the health arena. Allopathic doctors are beginning to talk about nutrition even though they were initially drug company trained. The time has come for each of us to learn the truth.

I try to keep my vision as clear as I can, considering both the present reality and the future. This is why I see an evolution, not a revolution in health care. 'The Powers That Be' have grown great control over humanity but they do not control all of us. Information, and their ability to withhold and obscure information, have been their method for exerting control over the world population throughout history. They seemed to come up with endless new ways to control us using cleverly-devised brainwashing techniques or even direct control. Let's not underestimate their intentions or their influence. The forces of truth and heart move ahead steadily, at their own pace. The powers that be do not own the whole of us. We can still dream, imagine and visualize. And as a person thinks, so they shall be.

My vision is that the many different practitioners of health and health care will soon talk to each other and that patients will become more responsible by taking the necessary preventative actions for themselves and their children. My vision is that humanity will develop a strong recognition of their inner power and take charge of their health. My vision is that humanity will investigate and study what matters most, leaving their passive tendencies behind them. As this progress slowly develops, planetary changes such as the quality of our air, water, and soil can improve. We cannot rush the seed as it grows into a plant. Visions are nice to have as long as we do what is necessary everyday to help them materialize into results through action.

The body dies. Whatever happens after that is a matter of personal belief. And if I was to speculate, without a body to change, the consciousness is free to connect to all, including the energy of what it is that we collectively create. Now is the time to shape our bodies to make the world itself a better, more healthful and holistic place. The world is holistic when you have the awareness and consciousness that it is holistic.

I give thanks from a place of heartfelt compassion for all that exists. I have wishes and dreams to help and serve humanity in the ways that I can. Join me in our evolution towards better health care. I ask that all who read this book — both professional and patient, because we are all patients—to remember one simple understanding: that we are all holistic human beings. All the organs of the body need each other for their best functioning. The body itself is a holistic team. Good health depends on a holistic concept in which we nurture all, because everything is affected by everything. The food we eat, the water we drink, our thoughts, ideas and emotions, our micro- and macro-biomes, etc.— each has an effect on the another. A helpful healing practitioner will always think in terms of the holistic picture, where diagnosis and treatment are holistic so that the patient can go back to focusing on prevention. We must work together to increase each others' consciousness; to live and practice holistically.

The Evolution

The doctor who gives drugs to suppress symptoms is causing the causes of disease to remain hidden and become worse, leading to more disease. What is needed is a lifestyle change.

www.lifestylepsychotherapy.com www.worldheartrevolution.com

APPENDIX

The following information is derived from my personal experiences with managing my health and is by no means a prescription for how anyone should live a healthful life. To live healthfully is a lifelong process that must be individually managed with help from your personal professional health care team. Read the following lists with a questioning mind and seek out your own best methods for maintaining your health.

Background Information About Dr. Walter J. Urban

Born in 1932

CCNY (Now CUNY) Psychology Major, BA 1949-1953

CCNY Educational Psychology, MA 1953-1954

CCNY Pre-Med, 1955-1956

University of Italy Bologna Medicine, 1956-1957

National Psychological Association for Psychoanalysis, Psychoanalyst, 1958-1966

Postgraduate Center for Psychotherapy, Community Consultant, 1966-1968

Family Institute, located in New York City, Family Therapy, 1969

Producer/host of TV program in New York City, <u>Psychoanalysis</u>, 1967. This was the first psychology program on TV.

International College, PhD Clinical Psychology, 1976-1979

Reposo Health Spa, Owner and Director, Desert Hot Springs, CA, 1981-1983

Energy of Life Institute of Costa Rica, Owner and Director, 2002-2017

Organic Farm Owner, 2009-present

Socrates Wellness Institute, Host, Perez Zeledon, Costa Rica, 2018-present

Author of:

Integrative Therapy: Foundation For Holistic And Self Healing (1978)

Do You Have The Courage To Change: The 12 Reasons Why You Don't Change And How You Can (2004)

Powerful Poems (2017)

Dr. Urban's personal lifetime dietary studies include courses and training in: the macrobiotic diet plan, Taoism, Buddhism, Polarity Therapy, Pulsor Therapy, raw food diet plan, juicing and juice fasting, colonics, ketogenic diet plan, paleo diet plan, vegetarian diet plan, vegan diet plan, and the Hippocrates program, etc.

Personal exercise studies include courses and training in: stretching, yoga, acupressure, meditation, Chinese face exercise, shamanism, spiritual healing, and more.

Dr. Urban offers a unique service of heart psychotherapy. this is for people who have various situations with their heart such as a cold heart, a frozen heart, a fearful heart, a disappointed heart, a lonely heart, a hateful heart, an unforgiving heart, a heartless heart, a foolish heart, a loveless heart, and more. Many people are unable to experience love, even though they long for it. The joy of the heart can be felt when the conditions are right and the blocks are removed. Visit his website for more information www. worldheartrevolution.com

Dr. Urban offers Unique Integrative Therapy (catered individually to each person) on Skype. You will learn how to detoxify your body, mind, emotions, thoughts and heart. You will be able to become peaceful with yourself and the world through learning patience, simplification, compassion, love and service. Help your spirit become free and flourish. This integrative therapy is a combination of psychoanalysis, taoism, buddhism, shamanism and other modalities combined in a unique way. It is possible to obtain results in one session. Contact doctorwalter123@gmail.com

Simplify: be healthy

It has taken me fifty years to unlearn my negative habits and put the new learning into practice that I have listed in this book. Even as I am writing, I am still learning to practice what I have learned. Practicing requires greater discipline than learning. I have had to learn to unlearn what I have been taught, and then put that into practice.

There are emotions connected directly or indirectly to the ideas that I was taught. I was taught that the ideas I was given were the correct ones. After all, my parents, teachers, religious leaders, culture, etc. were the best ones around and I did not have other options to learn from when I was a child. Since these ideas became a part of me, I learned to defend them. That's where the emotions began to enter. I learned how to believe that the ideas I was taught were part of who I am. My ideas became part of my character and I learned to use denial, avoidance, procrastination, anger, and so on to defend my beliefs and my very being.

Then, at age 14, I found a book on religion in the library and learned of other major religions. After reading it, I asked my father why my religion was better than the others? He did not have any answer that could satisfy me. I then began to wake up and question other things I was taught. I still maintained many other things I was taught, though, and I pursued them with a passion and great motivation almost every day of my life. I did not realize that I was also brainwashed by media, corporations, politicians, banks, and more. My life of obedience and acquisition became stronger and stronger. Little did I know, I was getting deeper and deeper into the lifestyle I was taught and becoming a type of slave to my ideas.

My deep, strong, hidden fears were not clearly known to me. They remained unconscious and guided most of my life. I was "normal" in many ways, doing what most people do. I became a slave to the system without the awareness that I was part of it. I could not see myself clearly as I pursued my goals and I could not see the world clearly, or all the hidden powers and forces behind the curtain. I did not understand how things really worked.

Since I was born in 1932, during the time of the great depression, my parents were jobless and poor. We lived on welfare stamps and food was very limited. Being very poor was a great teacher to me. I always say "thank you" for the great lesson I learned early in my life. At age four, I was on the street of The Bronx in New York City while my parents walked all over, looking for work.

My older sister would run away from me when I was left in her care and I quickly gained a sense of self-reliance at age four. I don't remember feeling any fear; I did whatever I had to do. Once again, I say "thank you." At age eight, I began my first business venture buying wholesale Tootsie Rolls and then reselling them at 100% profit. In a few months of selling them at Brighton Beach and Coney Island, I bought my first bicycle.

There are many more stories to be told, such as my one pair of shoes, or wearing my uncles too big clothes. Putting all my experiences together, I learned my survival depends on me, which I have found to be a good lesson to learn early in life. Once again, thank you. I had to learn early and quickly. My security depended on money and money came from my work and nowhere else. I became very motivated to survive and at age 16, I shared a room with a classmate and paid $7/week at 116 St. and Broadway in New York City.

After a lifetime of acquiring of material things, I learned to be a slave to the things I acquired. I needed to manage and maintain the things that I accumulated or I would lose them! After learning to be a good manager, my material things grew. This meant that I had even more to manage.

Then, in 1976, I moved to California where I attended many health lectures and began to become very interested in my health. Quite a change for me as a psychoanalyst, who was trained to think that health was all in the mind and emotions. My interest in health grew and grew and led me to 42 years of intensive studies and practices, which have brought me to this point of simplification.

Simplifying is a real challenge as we become more and more dependent on an ever-increasing technology to deal with our daily lives. Not only do we depend more on increasingly complex devices, but the great majority of us become addicted to the entertainment side of technology and the dopamine hits provided by things like social media validation. Our addictions become so strong that at times, people do not have normal conversations. We eat meals while watching smartphones and I have even seen someone brushing their teeth with one hand while watching their smartphone with the other. I do not judge these people because I have no right to do so. However, I wish they would take a look at themselves. It is difficult to simplify when one has no awareness that they have become victims to a type of controlled brainwashing. The easy path of passivity rather than taking of adult responsibility takes over. It becomes hard to observe yourself when you are enjoying yourself with passive entertainment.

Our collective brainwashing also extends to our health. We have learned that our health depends on doctors and drugs, rather than on ourselves and our personal responsibility over our everyday choices. The easy way is often chosen over the responsible way that requires effort and work. I woke up to this over four decades ago and I have watched many others wake up since. However, the majority are still asleep and dependent on the system. They lack motivation to change until they have a serious health crisis.

I hope that those of you who read this book will decide to make the changes you need now, before reaching a state of crisis. Good health practices are not complicated. The right thinking, food, exercise, sleep emotions and environment practiced every day make up the right lifestyle. Start today!

Creating A Better Life: From Seed To Fruition

Life is constant in challenge and change. Some of us can grow and flow with the river of change, while others sink into resistance and self-centered discontent.

With the courage to change, I embraced the higher consciousness of love, spirituality, and a raw food diet. When I read about the Hunzakuts' way of life in 1962, I became interested in nutrition, changing slowly from a regular diet of pizza, steak, cottage cheese, salami, Cheerios, French fries, chicken, and eggs; to fruit, vegetables, nuts and seeds. I did this gradually over a number of years and went through the usual "healing crisis" when I ate 100 percent raw food. I made strong, positive changes in my diet and the stored toxins had a chance to come out because I gave my the body good nutrition and took out the toxin-creating foods. And as a result, I experienced the various symptoms of the healing crisis, including headache, weakness, fatigue, and so on. These symptoms took place over months until I eliminated all of the toxins in my body and finally felt better.

I attended the City College of New York at age sixteen, where I obtained a B.A., an M.A., and became a premed student. I then attended the University of Bologna Medical School in Italy, but had to quit due to insufficient funds. I received my Ph.D. in Clinical Psychology in Los Angeles and my certificate in Psychoanalysis in New York City. I trained as a Mental Health Consultant at the Postgraduate Center For Psychotherapy in New York City and then trained as a Family Therapist. I became the Director of The Theodor Reik Consultation Center in New York City, then Clinical Director of the Transactional Analysis Training Institute in Beverly Hills. I had a private practice in Beverly Hills and New York City.

I own an organic farm in Costa Rica, where I now reside. I strove to spread the seeds of change by authoring the books: <u>Integrative Therapy: Foundations of Holistic and Self Healing</u> (1978), <u>Do You Have The Courage To Change?</u> (2004) and <u>Powerful Poems</u> (2017).

My meticulous diet and exercise routine keeps me going for twelve hours a day at the age of 87. I exercise six days a week and my outlook is decidedly positive. I am happy with my healthy, simple lifestyle. Sometimes, I have fruits in the morning and a large salad with avocado for dinner. With discipline you can change your lifestyle, prevent disease, gain more energy and strength, and look and feel good. You just have to make the decision and maintain your commitment to responsible choices.

My life has been devoted to helping myself and others. I practice what I preach, smile many times a day, and frequently affirm "I am peaceful" in my three-second meditations. In another, longer meditation period, I affirm: "I am healthy, strong, joyous, free, independent, protected, peaceful, loving, humble, forgiving, compassionate, truthful, part of nature," followed by an extra affirming: "Yes, I am." These affirmative meditations condition my cells and enhance my life. Try them with very little effort and no regrets!

I enjoy helping people who want to be informed and take responsibility for their lives. I am challenged by those who don't. Neither I, nor any other "doctor," can take over your responsibility for yourself.

Dr. Urban's Personal Daily Health Routine

1. When I have any health problems, I research them on the internet as much as possible before I go to the doctor. I go to see health care practitioners prepared with questions. In the past, if I was given any medications, I would check them on the internet before taking them. Now, I no longer take any pharmaceutical drugs but I do take natural herbs as remedies.
2. I have patience with the healing process and I keep a positive attitude. I silently talk to my problems, partly to ask them to heal

themselves, and partly to be aware of what I need to work on. I talk to my body and stay aware of the body's "intelligence" (its capacity to heal itself). I ask for help from the universal spiritual forces, too, as this helps me to stay aligned with my goals and intentions.

3. I practice good bowel management and have done three detoxification programs, as per Dr. Bernard Jensen's <u>Guide to Better Bowel Care: A Complete Program for Tissue Cleansing through Bowel Management</u>. On certain occasions when I need to, I take a herbal colon capsule and/or psyllium.

4. For many years now, I observe my levels of stress and frustration in different situations and to different people. I think about what it is in me that causes my reactions and I remember to tell myself that I am in control of my reactions, even if I cannot control anything else. As I do this, I practice maintaining control over my emotions, which I realize can hurt me. I prepare myself mentally for situations that I know to be frustrating to me. Sometimes, I silently say a mantra to myself, like "I am peaceful." If I feel that I am reacting emotionally, I put up my red flag reminder to quickly regain control. I realize that self-control is my job and that I cannot control the world around me. I don't expect others to change; the change must always be in me. It is my responsibility to myself to always realize that I must be in charge of myself. This self-awareness and action process has helped me avoid stress. I have faced my sickness, old age, and death, and I am not afraid, so I do not feel stress or frustration from these processes. Death is usually the biggest fear that people have, which is why I have studied various ideas that have freed me from this fear. Buddhism, shamanism, and various other forms of spirituality have all helped me to let go of fear and its consequence: stress.

5. I have developed the discipline to exercise 6 days a week. I started with a few minutes each day, which have increased to 1.5 hours daily. I do what I call 'Integrative Longevity Exercise.' I have developed this routine over the last 50 years of my life and it includes yoga, stretching, Chinese internal exercise, meditation, affirmations, pressure points, weights and freestyle tai chi.

6. My everyday mantra is: I am light energy, peaceful love and gratitude.

7. I say "thank you" many times during the day, I appreciate all that I have, and I try to simplify my life.

8. I place strong emphasis on love with my wife. I practice patience, love, compassion and understanding. I realize that we are all limited and that we each do the best that we can in the moment.

9. I focus as much as I can on the now — this moment — with mindfulness. I have personally had over 10 years of psychoanalysis, as well as group therapy, so I am relatively free from my past traumas and negative situations. I am constantly setting goals to achieve my best self, I am free from the fear of the future.

10. I have regular blood examinations performed to test my vitamin and mineral levels, making dietary changes and taking supplements where the results show that I need them. I prefer to increase my intake in foods that naturally supply the nutritional content that I require. My test results are amazingly good, so much so that I have been asked to give a talk to a group of doctors about my nutritional intake.

11. I very rarely use any pharmaceutical drugs. I have taken antibiotics once in my life for a stubborn Helicobacter pylori infection as it was an emergency situation. I use herbal remedies for my prostate, including some homeopathics.

12. I am constantly aware that I am a part of nature, even while I am living in the city of Medellin. I spend time outdoors and I meditate on my connection to all. I spend six months out of the year living on my farm in Costa Rica to ensure that I keep in balance with nature because I believe that we absorb healing energy from trees, bare ground, fresh air, nutritious food and filtered water.

13. I observe my thoughts and emotions to witness if my reactions contain the elements of egoist needs, which are those extending beyond my most essential needs and into the realm of greed, social status, and other highly egoic endeavors.

14. I rinse my mouth with hydrogen peroxide a few times a week.

15. I eat two tablespoons of coconut oil every day.

16. I sleep 8-9.5 hours every night, going to bed at 8pm at the latest.

17. My attitude and outlook toward life is positive and I live as much as possible in the moment through mindfulness practices. I enjoy my life and all that is in it, and I have an enduring 'never give up' point of view and I face up to who I am and what I can learn.
18. I listen with self-control and accept what is said, remaining open to learning at all times.
19. I set reasonable, achievable goals.
20. I have strong, creative desire to express myself through writing, poetry and painting.

Dr. Urban's Personal Diet Plan

I have practiced various diets in my 87 years, beginning with the Sad American Diet when I was growing up. As I learned and evolved, I switched to a macrobiotic diet, which progressed to a vegan diet. I also tried a vegetarian diet, raw food diet and twenty-two day fasts of just juicing. I have also learned the newest diet trends in the last few years from watching various diet summits on the internet (keto, paleo, Hippocrates, etc.) I learned that there is no one magic diet that is best suited to everyone or every situation.

I am currently focused on eating predominantly organic fruit, vegetables, nuts and seeds. I do not eat processed foods and I have recently excluded fish and chicken, which I ate sparingly before. I have eliminated sugar, fluoridated salt, carbonated drinks, animal milk and processed foods, which include coffee and alcohol. I use untreated salt made for animals, purchased in 45 kilo bags from the vet, and Himalayan salt. I do not eat animal products, other than the occasional free-range eggs for additional protein. My diet is mostly vegan and 70% raw food.

I have spent my life studying which foods contain which vitamins and minerals, as well as what my own body needs. I use various herbal teas as remedies. I have eliminated all hydrogenated vegetable oils (the bad oils) and use only coconut oil. I have evolved my own doubts about olive oil because of the false information. I make sure to eat avocado every day to get good fats into my diet. I used to eat wild salmon from Alaska for this same reason, as well as some sardines and clean-water, non-farm-raised fish, but I have recently gone back to a strictly vegan, mainly raw food diet.

I practice food combining. Put simply, this means that I do not eat carbohydrates and proteins together, fruit is eaten alone, and vegetables are eaten with either carbohydrates or proteins — never both.

Sugar substitutes come under about 35 different names, including aspartame, sweet and low, dextrose, sucrose, etc., so I carefully read dietary information before I buy anything deceptive, like fruit juice. The best way to avoid hidden ingredients is to avoid packaged or processed foods and beverages wherever possible.

I eat some "good" nuts like walnuts, macadamia and pistachio. I have also started to eliminate all the "no" foods listed in Dr. Gundry's book, The Plant Paradox (2017), and to eat all of the 'yes' foods.

Even after all of this, I do not have a perfect diet because I eat in restaurants some of the time. I continue making good choices wherever possible and move forward with good health in mind, including continuously training myself to prepare the most nutritious meals possible.

"When I Eat, I…"

1. Chew and chew and chew
2. Eat slowly
3. Enjoy the food
4. Stop when ¾ full
5. Stop drinking 20 minutes before eating and start hours later, depending on the meal
6. Eat in good company (not with screens)
7. No cold food in stomach
8. Use good salt (untreated)
9. Use good oils (no vegetable oils)
10. Eat an early dinner (no later than 6pm)

11. Eat at regular times
12. No sugar (or substitutes)
13. No processed food
14. Eat kale and all green leafy vegetables
15. Eat organically grown foods
16. No red meat or pork, chicken or fish

Thirty Proverbs For A New Outlook On Life

1. The wise person knows that he is powerless. That is his power.
2. The strength of silence affords the opportunity to learn.
3. Forget who you were to become who you are.
4. You own nothing.
5. Self-development is your main job.
6. Enlightenment is an illusion.
7. Clean your mind so that you can clean your house.
8. Look inside so that you can see the outside clearly.
9. Open your mind to learning rather than repeating what you think you know.
10. Improving patience adds days to your life.
11. Learning how to learn is the first thing to learn.
12. Don't defend your beliefs so that you can open your mind.
13. Your biggest enemy is your closed mind.
14. Your emotions can prevent your use of logic.
15. Don't blame your emotions; understand their origin.
16. Emotional people need your understanding if you can give it.
17. Practicing calmness builds strength.
18. When you are ready to give up, remember your inner strength.
19. Wisdom can grow from your own thinking.
20. Your parents did their best.
21. Say thanks every day.
22. Do what you know is right; not what makes you feel good.
23. You are responsible and no one else is responsible for you.
24. If you pay more attention to your health than your wealth, you will live longer.

25. Patience is not just waiting—it is waiting calmly.
26. Self-observation is needed for self-control.
27. Following norms will make you a slave and rob your freedom.
28. Gossip gains nothing and wastes energy.
29. Every fight has two losers.
30. If you think before you speak, you will speak less.

Energy For Self-Healing

Everything is made of energy. The Life Force that brings everything together is made of energy. We need energy to live. The food we eat both consumes and creates energy. Waste needs energy to be removed. Live food has energy. Cooked food takes more energy to digest than live food. Processed food requires more energy to digest than cooked food. Drugs and excess hormones release toxins in the body and energy is required to process and eliminate them. Toxins are eliminated through the skin, lungs, colon, kidneys, bladder and lymphatic system. Despite all of this, corporations are still allowed to promote devitalized, packaged, pre-cooked, chemically-processed, growth hormone-filled food. All thoughts, feelings and emotions require energy. What happens when we obtain our energy from polluted sources? Our cells need energy to function and mitochondria produce energy. Energy is the foundation of all life. The body functions best with harmony and balance of energy.

Energy is directed by thought. Blockages of energy create imbalance and disharmony leading to disease. Thoughts are directing energy in our bodies and negative thoughts make for imbalances in our internal energy flow. With thoughts in mind, I have created a special meditative exercise which I practice everyday. The purpose is to create a strong energy for healing; a concentration of energy, which I then focus on my body, with special attention directed at the parts that need healing so that I can strengthen my life force energy. I focus my mind's energy on the following steps while moving my hands into certain positions, which I will not describe here as they would be better served demonstrated. I use this process to concentrate and gather energy forces available from the following sources:

- The body's ability to heal itself using the body's intelligence
- My personal spirit guides
- The cosmic and universal energy
- God Force Energy combined with my internal energy force (as described in Buddhism)
- The energy of positive belief
- The vision of the future outcome (how I will be, I am that now)
- The chakras
- The mitochondria
- The telomeres
- The endocrine glands
- Heart pumping energy
- The sun's energy

I use all of these energies and focus them into one, unified, powerful force to be applied to each part of my body in need of special attention for healing. This is followed by a series of Chinese finger tapping exercise on my body's meridians and Chinese face exercises, which connect the energy I have harvested and directs it towards my organs. All of the above exercises are part of a larger program called Integrative Longevity Exercise, which I practice six days a week.

This meditative exercise of energy for healing needs discipline and patience to learn and practice. I am happy to teach it to those motivated to become stronger and to attain optimal health.

Love, The Energy Of Light

From the sun comes the light. We have an inner light, too, which comes from us as much as it comes from the sun. Light is a form of energy; never created, never destroyed. With light energy comes love. Many will tell you to love yourself first and then you can love others. For me, love is not separate.

When you love, the energy of that love becomes universal because love does not have limits. It is an energy that loves everything. When you love your mate, you also love the trees and everything else. Understanding this depends on your level of consciousness. If you are limited by the state of your ego, you may not understand this. Developing more consciousness enhances the ability to love. Accepting the world with love is not passive because love is an active energy that enhances understanding. And understanding enhances love.

There Is Always Light

Sometimes we don't see the light, feel the light or think the light. When this happens, we remain with the other thoughts, feelings and emotions that we are experiencing. If you consider that we are all vibrations of light energy and that these vibrations are the foundations of who we are, then there is always light because we are light. When we hold this belief in mind, we can always see the light.

What light means may differ from person to person and for many it is a positive idea. Experiencing light can give us hope when we are surrounded by darkness. The energy of hope is a positive force. When we really have faith in hope, the light gets turned on, even when it is not thought, felt or seen. It all begins with how you think. This is the universal experience of being human, even when seeing and feeling cannot unite us in our experience. When you think light, you increase the feeling of light internally. Think it, and it will always be there. You are the light, your own light, the universal light, and your thinking connected to it. You may choose to say to yourself, "I am light."

Planetary Prophecy Fool, Or Taoist?

To those of you who have a fuller realization of what is going on; to those who hold valuable information and to the truth seekers who have a boundless curiosity: it is important to be aware that even with the vast, secret, technological capabilities of the world's superpowers (corporations and nation states), nature will always triumph.

Some have predicted that a revolution will occur in the near future in the US and that it will become a third world country that will submit to an overarching world government and accept a world currency, known as Special Drawing Rights (SDRs), which will become a BANCOR, which is a new type of currency that we can expect to see regularly in our future. Multinational corporations, central banks, the World Bank and IMF could continue to push their agendas out of greed, causing more people to die, starve or get sick. Eventually, we will begin to realize that no matter how things evolve, we need the planet to produce food for our survival. Self-destructive mechanisms of food production such as GMO seeds and food production have had backlash that will continue to grow. Food is the foundation of society and we cannot eat gold, petroleum or currencies.

All sides (separations) are fighting desperately to achieve their goals. Each of them believe that the outcome can be controlled by their powers. The Taoist, on the other hand, believes in the Great Way, where the laws of nature reign high.

The basic instinct of all species is survival according to the laws of nature and Monsanto has showed us that their weed killer has now caused a new weed that is about two meters tall. Perhaps this is a an example or lesson of the power of nature and that those who survive the in the future will evolve into a new type of human being, one of heart, love and compassion!

A Series Of Poems, By Dr. Walter J. Urban

Heart Revolution

Heart revolution
Love is solution
You must look inside
Let love be your guide
Learn how to do it

Slowly, bit by bit
Take all time you need
Learn to plant the seed
The seed of your love
Fed by rain above
Fed by earth below
Let your good heart show
Let in sunshine, too
See the best in you
It's always been there
Behind the cold stare
Love is solution
New revolution

Good Old Days

The good old days
The good old ways
Used to be fun
Now it's cop's gun
We used to dance
And have romance
We used to talk
Go for a walk
Now it's cell phones
And killer drones
Planes go faster
War disaster
Think back a while
Days of the smile
Beautiful tunes
Beware the goons
And as you sit
Your teeth you grit
What will come next
Message in text

Implant your chip
Go on drug trip
Looking for peace
Wars never cease
You sit and wait
Search for your mate
As the world turns
And no one learns
To stop and see
How you could be
The good old ways
The good old days

My World

You are my world
My love unfurled
I see your smile
Once in a while
Then I feel good
Just like I should
Each day love more
Open soul's door
And there I find
Such peace of mind
And there I stay
Please come by way
And be with me
For can't you see
You are my world
Your love unfurled

Only Love

Yes, only love
Lights from above

Shines in us all
The short the tall
Our relations
All the nations
The trees and the birds
Animal herds
The earth the sky
Wonder not why
It's all so clear
Life without fear
Love in the heart
Every day's start
When you awake
First breath you take
Light from above
It's only love

Illusion

Life's illusion
Your confusion
You chase your dream
Then it does seem
You've reached your goal
You've paid the toll
Then you awake
And try to take
Another look
At a new book
And there you find
Another kind
A new idea
It becomes clear
You think you know
New way to go
Again you try

New kind of sigh
Only to find
You are blind
New confusion
Life's illusion

My Love

A warm embrace
A smiling face
Hearts that meet
What a treat
To have you near
My lovely dear
To make you real
My love to feel
Oh, where are you now?
I'll find you somehow
Looking here and there
Looking everywhere
More than a dream
Our love will seem
To be so warm
Your lovely form
Your beautiful eyes
Your good mind, so wise
As you appear
I lose my fear
Of not finding you
My love has come true
With your smiling face
And your warm embrace

Printed in the United States
By Bookmasters